AIRLINE

THE INSIDE STORY
OF BRITISH AIRWAYS

AIRLINE

THE INSIDE STORY OF BRITISH AIRWAYS

ARTHUR REED

BBC BOOKS

Published by BBC Books,
a division of BBC Enterprises Limited
Woodlands, 80 Wood Lane, London W12 0TT

First published 1990
© Arthur Reed 1990
ISBN 0 563 20718 3

Set in 11/13pt Garamond by Phoenix Photosetting, Chatham
Printed and bound in England by Mackays of Chatham PLC, Chatham, Kent
Jacket printed by Belmont Press Limited, Northampton

CONTENTS

PREFACE

International air travel was born on 25 August 1919 when one passenger climbed into a converted First World War bomber to be flown from London to Paris. The aircraft had a top speed of 121 mph. The pilot, wearing helmet, goggles and a leather jacket to protect him from the elements as he sat in the open cockpit of the canvas-and-wood biplane, navigated his way to the coast by following the railway line, and by reading the names of the stations painted on their roofs.

Seventy years on, one billion passengers fly on the world's airlines in each twelve-monthly period, a large proportion of them in jumbo jets carrying over 400 at a time; a select few in the supersonic Concorde, racing the sun at 1350 mph at altitudes as high as 55 000 feet. The aircraft are made of steel, titanium, aluminium and increasingly of carbon-fibre composite materials. Their pilots, relaxed in shirt-sleeves on their air-conditioned flight-decks, navigate by using information supplied to them by on-board computers, which present them with this and all the other vital information which they need, on seven-colour cathode-ray tube screens.

By any yardstick, this has been a remarkable progress over a relatively short period of time. Inevitably, such galloping expansion has not been achieved without problems. Many airlines begun by optimistic pioneers and aviation idealists have been blown out of existence by the cold winds of economic reality. There have been amalgamations, as the trend towards a small number of mega-carriers accelerated. British Airways, the subject of this book, which can trace its lineage back to that first flight in 1919, has had its crises, but has now emerged to be one of the world leaders of a volatile industry whose profitability can be affected more than most others by the cyclical trends of travel patterns influenced by the strength of currencies, oil prices, wars and rumours of wars.

Running a big modern airline is a fascinating, frustrating, rewarding and highly-complex business in which the skills of the economist, the financier, the marketeer and the computer wizard are equally as important as those of the engineer and the pilot. Unlike the can of beans on the supermarket shelf, the airline seat is a highly-perishable commodity which, if not sold on the day of flight, cannot be offered in the marketplace tomorrow. Making certain that the right number of seats are sold, and at the right price, is increasingly the task of the computer, a device which is going to play a central role in determining where the line is drawn between the red and the black figures in the industry's accounts, and its ability to survive in the future.

Although it touches upon the early days of the airline industry, *Airline* is more concerned with the recent history of British Airways. The merger between British European Airways and British Overseas Airways Corporation, the move from the public to the private sector and the cliff-hanging coming together of British Airways and British Caledonian Airways (BA called it a merger; most others termed it a takeover) are the central events.

Interleaved with this series of headline-catching events are descriptions of the everyday aspects of the work of a major airline. We follow, from the cockpit, a scheduled flight from London to Rome and back, we learn how the engineers regularly defy the force of gravity to keep the aircraft flying safely, we read how the marketeers sell the seats and the freight capacity, and keep the 'image' of the airline in the public eye. And we study how British Airways uses computers, a business tool which has made possible the enormous growth in recent years of the entire airline industry.

Finally we look into the future of civil aviation. Will it be some time in the next century that BA passengers arrive overhead Sydney, Australia, one hour after leaving London via some form of sub-orbital flight vehicle? Against the background of the progress which aviation has made over the past seventy years, it would be a brave pundit indeed who dismissed this concept as impossible.

Arthur Reed

CHAPTER ONE

WHERE THE BIG BIRDS ROOST

British Airways is a big airline, but it has pretensions towards becoming far bigger. In the world airline league table for 1988, it was rated twelfth in passenger-carrying – with 24.6 million customers – and tenth in fleet size, with 204 aircraft.

BA's management believes that it is only by being numbered among the ranks of the so-called 'mega' airlines that it will successfully survive in the future. And a major concern is the fact that there were eleven airlines who carried more passengers than BA in 1988.

BA's urge to move up the table is the reason why its management prowls the airline scene looking for deals which could produce new partners and inflate its size. It was also the motivation behind the takeover of British Caledonian, the long pursuit of a 20% stake in the Belgian state airline Sabena, and the unsuccessful attempt in 1989 to become a shareholder in United.

A constant irritant, however, and a block to BA's expansionist ethos is the attitude of the US government which has so far prevented BA obtaining a significant holding in any major US airline. Lord King, the BA Chairman, told American businessmen in Washington DC at the end of 1989, 'If I am not allowed to buy a US airline, I shall object to a US company buying a British airline – or, for that matter, any other within the European Community.'

While BA frets about its stature up against the American airlines, those which are below it in the league table (like Lufthansa and Japan Airlines) worry about the extent of the commercial muscle BA already possesses today, and what they consider the arrogant manner in which it sometimes flexes that muscle to get its way. These worries have surfaced in particular among the other big national airlines in Europe, all of which remain state-owned, or partially so, while BA has gained its freedom through privatisation. For though public ownership may offer the advantage of financial security, it also seriously inhibits the making of important strategic decisions – such as the re-equipping of airliner fleets – because of the need to refer these decisions to government.

Some of the smaller UK-based airlines are concerned that, in its privatised state, BA has become so powerful as to dominate the airline and airports scene. When the deal with Sabena was being lined up to give BA a foot in the 'hub' airport at Brussels, Michael Bishop, Chairman of the Airlines of Britain Group which includes British Midland Airways, objected that it would give BA an unfair, monopolistic advantage.

Bishop made it clear that he would seek, through the European Community Monopolies and Mergers Commission, to have some of BA's take-off 'slots' at Heathrow revoked. British Midland, the second busiest operator at Heathrow after BA, flies head-to-head against BA on the main British trunk routes, and was expected to suffer when BA revamped its shuttle product during 1989. But Michael Bishop claimed that during this period his trunk route traffic actually increased.

'The new shuttle has not been anything like as successful as BA hoped,' he said. 'Our core customers have remained remarkably loyal to us.'

Other airlines in more distant parts of the world also remain suspicious of BA's good intentions. BWIA is the biggest airline in the Caribbean, and its Chairman, Karl Hudson-Phillips QC, alleged obstructionism by BA in the matter of BWIA's operations in its own region.

'All we are asking for is parity with BA, which holds traffic rights to eight Caribbean countries,' he said. 'Yet it is this equal competition that has been vigorously resisted for so long.' Such protection of the BA monopoly on several Caribbean routes, and the inhibition of frequency on others, is in marked contrast to the stated British policy of freedom of airline competition, and BA's own well-publicised welcoming of competition on any route.

So what sort of company has BA become since it was turned around financially from what US management expert Peter Keen described in his book *Competing In Time* (Ballinger, 1988) as, 'An airline within 48 hours of bankruptcy, and with a reputation for service whose quality and style used to match that of British cooking'?

There is no doubt that it has improved considerably since the condition outlined by Keen. Now financially buoyant (pre-tax profit for the six months ended 30 September 1989 was a record £259 million), it is seeking to develop its own 'style', and this is the imponderable which differentiates one big long-haul airline from another in an age when they all fly the same airliner types over the same routes and from the same airports.

All have their own first-class cabins in the airliners, and first-class lounges on the ground, their own business classes, their own children's travel clubs, their own operations rooms where a watch is maintained on the progress of the fleet 24 hours a day, 365 days a year. It takes a frequent, professional traveller to tell one major airline from another these days. In this chapter we chart a 'day in the life' of BA as it and its workers try to live up to the advertising boast that it is 'the world's favourite', sometimes getting it right and sometimes falling far short of the lofty aspirations which the management under Lord King has built up.

Terminal 4, Heathrow airport, fifteen miles to the west of London, is the nest to which British Airways' big birds always return to roost. But reversing the natural habits of the feathered species, the airline's Boeing 747s, Lockheed TriStars and, occasionally, McDonnell Douglas DC–10s (the natural habitat of the DC–10 is BA's second London base at Gatwick) come home in the morning and fly away again during the day.

It is 5 am on a day in midsummer, and the first of the brood has just alighted on Heathrow's runway 28 Left with a delicacy which belies the fact that she weighs around 300 tons fully loaded. During the previous day and night, at speeds of over 500 mph and a height of 35 000 feet, the 747 has tracked its way from Seoul in South Korea to Tokyo, and then across the northern Pacific ocean and the Bering Sea for a refuelling stop in Anchorage, Alaska, changing crews on the way. On its final leg towards London, it crossed over the Beaufort Sea, just south of the North Pole, across Greenland, north of Iceland, until making a landfall on the north-west coast of Scotland. Now it is earthbound again, rumbling across the concrete at a cautious 5 mph, nodding gently as the undercarriage comes up against the joins between the slabs. All the airborne grace has vanished. As somebody put it succinctly – avoiding the bird analogy, it looks for all the world like a mansion on roller skates.

The final few feet of this transcontinental journey are literally inch by inch, as the crew on the high flight-deck line up with the panel on the terminal wall which tells them precisely when and where to stop. The main forward door comes to a halt precisely in line with the air bridge down which the passengers will disembark, and the gap between aircraft and the terminal is closed when the bridge is extended against the fuselage. This operation, too, demands skills; the air-bridge operator has to take a driving test before he is allowed at the controls, for anything other than the lightest of kisses on the fuselage could result in a bent aircraft, costly repairs, and hundreds of thousands of pounds of lost revenue while it is out of service.

The bridge-operator lends a hand to the crew inside the aircraft to open the massive door. As it swings on its hinges, a blast of warm air bearing a strong but indefinable smell wafts out. One of the team of BA people poised on the bridge hazards a guess at its constituent parts – 'part aviation, hot hydraulic fluid, and so on, part the croissants which were served for breakfast, and part human beings; after all, over 300 of them have been locked up inside that metal tube together for a very long time'.

First out of the aircraft is the company mail, followed closely by the first-class passengers, the rest of the 300 being blocked discreetly by the cabin crew until those who have paid the premium fare have gone. Then the long procession begins in earnest, people of all colours, races, religions, social classes, with a thousand different reasons for their journey, but all of whose destinies have been united for a few hours. Without exception, they and their clothes look crumpled; a few of them stumble a little as the stiffness begins to leave their joints after their long sojourn in a sitting position.

BA staff are there to try to pick out three particular passengers from the 300. While the 747 was in flight, telex messages have alerted the arrivals staff to the fact that one traveller needs a wheelchair, one has a problem with his ticket, one is elderly and on his own and requires guidance towards the onward flight on which he is booked. As the passengers begin to move towards the door, the names of the three are put over the aircraft's public-address system. First, the invalid identifies himself and climbs into a waiting wheelchair. Then comes the man with the ticket problem, an obviously well-travelled business executive, who is used to problems while moving around the airways. He has, he is told, the wrong coupon – no fault of his – but would he go to the appropriate BA ticket desk to have the matter sorted out. 'Well,' he says, amazingly good-humoured after his night in the air, 'I thought I'd heard everything about this flying business, but this is a new one on me.' Finally the elderly passenger makes himself known, a man with hardly any English and plainly bewildered by the unfamiliar scene.

Last to leave the jumbo are the cabin staff, still cheerful but some showing signs of fatigue on their faces after their all-night stint looking after the wants of their charges. On the ground below, separate BA teams unload the passengers' baggage (first-class luggage comes out and is put on to the carousels in the baggage hall first), extract the containers holding the freight, hauling them off to the airline's massive cargo centre a mile further along the airport, empty the waste tanks, replenish the water, carry out an engineering check, rectifying any minor defects on which the flight crew have filed reports, and a hundred and one other tasks. The aircraft is due to leave on another intercontinental journey in a few hours' time, and the business of winding it down from one flight overlaps with preparations for the next. A group of cleaners go through the cabin (which, at the end of a long-haul service, looks as if it has been the venue for a camping-out party, with pillows and blankets strewn everywhere and empty glasses tucked into every crevice) to a pre-set programme which has a stop-watch precision. Once the amazing amount of detritus has been cleared away – as much as half a ton from airliners which have completed very long sectors – the carpets are vacuumed, the ashtrays emptied, the seat tables polished, the toilets cleaned and disinfected. The aircraft is restocked with clean blankets and pillows, and with headrest covers – 'dressing' the cabins, as it is called.

Six-thirty am, and Terminal 4 has swallowed the passengers from the Tokyo flight as if they never existed. Apart from an unhappy few still in deep discussion with customs or immigration, they have claimed their luggage and passed from the 'airside' of the terminal to 'landside'. The overhead television screens giving notice of arriving flights are now becoming busy as other BA airliners approach home base from distant corners of the world. Five jumbo jets come in before 5.30 am each day, and imminent arrivals are posted from Melbourne via Singapore, from Peking via Hong Kong, from Delhi via Kuwait, from Mauritius via Bahrain, from JFK New York, from Johannesburg, from São Paulo via Rio de Janeiro, from Pittsburgh via Philadelphia and, more prosaically, from Paris and Amsterdam (Terminal 4 is used by BA for these two short-haul routes; the remainder use Terminal 1 in the airport's central area). Terminal 4 is not a 'quiet' terminal – that is, with no spoken announcements – as is the case in some other parts of the world, but the airline and the owners/operators, Heathrow Airport Ltd, try to keep the noise down as much as possible. Even so, there is at this time of day a string of calls for arriving passengers to go to the meeting point, interspersed with repetitions of the security message, 'May we remind all passengers not to leave their baggage unattended at any time'.

Seven am, and in a small, windowless room behind the scenes in the terminal, BA's supervisory staff assemble for their regular morning meeting to review the events of the previous day and anticipate the day ahead. The airline's terminal manager is in the chair but the atmosphere is very informal, with coffee on the boil and little rank in evidence. Heads of various departments sketch in their scenes. Staffing levels are down that day because of sickness. Several departing flights have been labelled with the 'security' tag since they are bound for politically sensitive parts of the world. Two departing flights have been designated 'red', ten 'amber', the rest 'green' – a reference to the numbers of seats available on each: red means that there is little chance of late ticket-buyers getting aboard, amber that such a state is being approached, green that there is room to spare. In the case of a red flight there may be more passengers than seats, in which case staff must face up to the chore of telling customers that they are being moved into a different class of travel from that which they have booked, or at worst that they are being offloaded. But before that happens volunteers will be asked for among the passengers to stop over for the next flight; compensation is paid to those who agree, and at £200 for twenty-four hours there is usually no shortage of takers among those who have time to spare.

Peak time for that morning is predicted as being 10 am. There are going to be two late-arriving aircraft, one due to a technical delay at New Delhi, the other because a crew in some distant spot has run out of the hours they are legally allowed to fly before having to rest. Around 1100 of the arriving passengers are due to transfer to other flights and so will not go outside the airport. There are heavy bookings to the United States because of a low-fare offer which has just been publicised by the marketing people. BA's Special Services department (a small group whose role is to take care of the airline's VIPs and/or CIPs – commercially important passengers) reports that it will be looking after a number of important bankers on their way to an International Monetary Fund meeting. Balancing to some extent the earlier news of overbookings, another supervisor reports a high level of 'no-shows' – customers who have booked seats, but do not turn up to claim them; although it has talked about it for years, the airline industry has not so far been able to agree a scheme which would penalise such action. Staff standing by in the hope of taking up the concessionary travel to which they are entitled are reported in considerable numbers, but in spite of the no-shows few of them look as if they are going to be lucky that day.

With the problems of the hours ahead identified, the meeting turns to the previous day's events, highlighted by the breakdown of one of the baggage belts. 'I reckon our staff did a terrific job under pretty harrowing circumstances,' says one of the supervisors, who had been in the thick of the resulting chaos. A further continuing worry for the airline – and like the baggage belts out of its control – is the long queues at 'central search', the line of security-screening posts through which all passengers using the terminal must pass with the hand baggage which they intend to take on to the aircraft, after they have shown their boarding cards to prove that they are going to travel. Following the Lockerbie disaster in which a Pan American 747 was blown up by a bomb with the loss of all lives on board, security at Heathrow was tightened considerably, with the result that a far higher proportion of passengers than before had their hand luggage subjected to a physical search after it had been through the X-ray machines. The previous day it had taken some travellers up to two hours to queue for central search, so that departure schedules were in serious danger of disruption.

The meeting discusses giving priority for screening, which is carried out by Heathrow Airport Ltd but overseen by Government, to passengers whose flights are due to leave first. 'The trouble is', says one of the supervisors, 'that although the airline is not responsible, baggage belts and security are a British Airways problem as far as most of our passengers are concerned.' Those at the meeting are asked to watch out for early signs that the lines for security may swell during the day ahead. 'We want to be pro-active and anticipate the problems, rather than re-active – sorting out the problems after they have happened,' the terminal manager comments.

After just a quarter of an hour the meeting breaks up, but representatives from it go straight on to a second meeting which, this time, is formed of people from most of the other departments within the airline (including engineering, cleaning, operations) who are involved in the drive for on-time arrival and departure of services. Heathrow management is also present and reports that yesterday's belt problem has been solved. Engineering, however, warns that there are some significant snags on two services, including an undercarriage defect which will have to be looked at. As a result there will be no spare aircraft that day. Once again the atmosphere is informal, but at the same time businesslike; the meeting closes after a short time with those attending scattering to their tasks all over the airport. 'Have a fun day, folks,' says the chairman as they go.

Nine am, and things are beginning to peak for British Airways in Terminal 4. The first passengers for the airline's blue riband departure, the 10.30 am supersonic Concorde flight to New York (accorded the flight number 001 in recognition of the prestige which attaches to it), are coming in, most of them changing from other flights which have left European capitals earlier that day. They check in at special desks, which are decked out with vases of flowers (other first-class and club passengers also receive the flower treatment). Passengers joining the Concorde flight from their homes or offices around London often cut their check-in to the last moment. Most of them are regulars and know the ropes; one businessman uses the service once a week throughout the year.

Having gone through the formalities at the desk, the Concorde travellers are invited to use BA's Speedwing lounge on the other side of immigration and the security checks, a haven of peace in a bustling terminal which they share with other passengers holding first-class tickets. The facilities there include drinks and snacks, newspapers and magazines, comfortable armchairs and settees, and phones for those last-minute calls which most international business people seem to find it vital to make. The wide windows of the lounge look out over the airport and, in particular, the sleek white shape of the Concorde in which they are to fly, having the final touches put to it before the call for boarding. And when that comes the Concorde élite, who (or whose companies) have paid in excess of £4000 for the return journey to New York in half the time taken by the subsonic jets, walk on board through an air bridge directly from the lounge.

The Speedwing is one of a cluster of lounges which BA operates for the benefit of various groups of passengers in Terminal 4. There is one for Club World and Club Europe passengers, and another for the airline's Executive Club Members. Then there is the Oasis, for passengers who have long stopovers at Heathrow between flights. It is used largely by travellers from the Middle East changing planes in London on their way to or from North America, and its ambience pays service to their particular demands: there are showers, the buffet has ethnic foods, and there is an area set aside for prayers. In the case of lengthy lay-overs between flights, BA will organise a stay at one of the many hotels around the perimeter of the airport which offer day rooms. The Skyflyers' lounge caters for children, all of whom are automatically made members of BA's 'Skyflyers' Club' when they travel with the airline, with various little perks like a log book and badges. Activity in this lounge comes to a peak at school holiday time, when hundreds of youngsters – 'most of them very experienced travellers, and very independent,' says a BA man – pass through the airport on the way from their schools in Britain to join their parents who are living and working abroad. Facilities in the Skyflyers cater for the special needs of this group, and include comic books, pop videos, squash, and potato chips.

BA carries some 14 000 children travelling on their own each year (they used to be termed 'unaccompanied minors', but that rather bureaucratic description has now been dropped), and will take special care of them up to the age of sixteen. A group of 150 BA staff, both men and women, whose normal jobs cover a wide spectrum of activities, from nursing to check-in, volunteer to use part of their off-duty time to accompany children on flights. Each one looks after ten at a time, softening the parting with their parents, occupying the time during the journey, guiding them through the destination airport, and handing them over to whoever is meeting them at the other end. The volunteers are appointed only after a careful vetting by the airline, including putting them in with groups of children to assess their compatibility.

On the aircraft, each Skyflyer is given an 'activities pack', containing games and colouring sets, and a special menu listing such delectables as hamburgers and beans, and bangers and mash. Over long-haul journeys, close friendships are struck up between the children and their escorts, with names and addresses and autographs exchanged as the flight comes in to land. Escort-led community singing is not unknown, and there is a story within BA that the first-class cabin on one airliner where this was happening complained – not because they objected to the noise but because they had not been invited to join in.

Ten am, and BA's teams of hunters are in full cry as the pace in Terminal 4 rises to a frenzy. Hunters are a recent addition to the airline's passenger-service portfolio, uniformed men and women, identifiable by the red carnation in their buttonholes, who have no geographical boundaries within the terminal, and whose role, as explained by one of their supervisors, is 'to find the passenger with a problem, before they bring that problem to us'. Their task has an obvious public-relations flavour to it also, for a helping hand for a passenger who is looking lost will, BA hopes, send that passenger away with an image of BA as a 'caring' airline. So how often are the red carnations changed? 'Don't tell anybody, but they're made of silk. But they are renewed fairly often.'

Along the terminal's vast concourse an unusual passenger is being checked in for a flight to New York, although not too unusual, as BA reckons it carries 200 dogs on its services out of Heathrow each week. This one is a greyhound, and to match its aerodynamic profile it is accommodated in a long, thin carrying container, the specifications for which are laid down in a lengthy series of regulations issued to the airlines by the International Air Transport Association (IATA). In the past, pets – and BA transports, in addition to dogs, countless cats, hamsters, tortoises, gerbils, budgerigars, and even snakes, worth in all some £2 million in business a year – had to go through the airline's cargo centre, but now, always providing they are in the correct housing, they can be checked in as excess baggage by their owners, and travel in the underfloor holds of the same airliner. The hold generally used for this traffic is to the rear of the airliner and is pressurised and heated. Most pets do not seem to worry over the experience; BA's advice to owners is that their pets need not be sedated for the journey, although counsel ought to be taken from the vet who usually attends the animal which is due to take a trip. The airline likes the scheme, not only for its revenue-producing potential, but because it discourages the practice in which a few of its customers indulge of smuggling small pets on board concealed in their handbags or inside their coats. The practice is anti-social for both human and animal flyers, dangerous from the point of view of air safety, and illegal under regulations designed to control rabies. The greyhound in his container is whisked away to be loaded on board, thus qualifying for membership of another of BA's groups, the Flying Pets Club, which brings with it a 'passport' in which the peripatetic quadruped's aerial journeys may be recorded.

Eleven am, and in the BA operations room, tucked away in the Queen's Building in the central area of the airport, operations staff are not only monitoring closely the comings and goings of airliners at Terminal 4, but also at the airline's stations all over the world. Somebody once likened them to spiders sitting in the centre of a web, and the comparison is a nice one for, at the slightest tremor of trouble coming in from anywhere on the BA network, be it in Aberdeen, Scotland, or Auckland, New Zealand, they pounce on it, with the aim of sorting the trouble out. The ops director sums up the role: 'Supposing the airline was running completely smoothly, then we really have nothing to do, but when things start to go wrong, our job is to manage disruption, to co-ordinate all the activities needed to put things right again, and to reduce delays with the least possible inconvenience to the passengers.'

Their task is a complicated and a tough one, going on as it does round the clock in shifts, 365 days a year. Short/medium-haul services, mainly within Britain and into mainland Europe, are somewhat easier to manage than long-haul, with the fleet flying between 6 am and 10 pm and then returning to base at Heathrow for overnight maintenance. If the operation has been disrupted during any one day for any reason – and bad weather and air traffic control congestion are the two most likely ones – it can usually be recovered reasonably easily the following day, with a fresh sheet of paper ready to be filled in from six o'clock in the morning.

Conversely, the long-haul operation never ends for there are always BA airliners in the air somewhere, with others preparing to take off or land. Forty of the foreign stations to which the airline flies have night curfews – that is, they do not allow aircraft to operate during the small hours. Fitting the flights around these is part of a giant jigsaw puzzle which must, at times, always seem to have a piece missing. The operations team is geared to making quick decisions about situations which may be happening 10 000 miles away, considering options A, B and C, and probably D, E and F as well.

The weather forecasters tell them that a 747 en route for Hong Kong will arrive as the tail of a typhoon passes through, making a landing at Kai Tak, in normal conditions a tricky airport to negotiate, impossible. The designated alternate is a fairly basic place in mainland China, but by that time the flight crew will be out of hours, and there are certainly not enough hotels in the area to look after the 300 passengers on board. Thinking on their feet, the ops people at Heathrow make the decision to divert the flight into Bangkok, where they know there is plenty of accommodation and where they can find a spare crew if it becomes necessary. Pilots, flight engineers and cabin crew are switched and reswitched about the world to help smooth such situations, transported by local airlines or, if there are none available and the need is urgent, specially chartered aircraft. Hurricanes in the Caribbean, monsoons in India, insurrections somewhere else, an aircraft that goes sick on the ground somewhere on the west coast of America in the middle of the British night – all set the adrenalin flowing in ops control in London and call for speedy decisions which, if made wrongly, can cost the airline a lot of money and the loss of a lot of goodwill.

The 'knock-on' effect of delays on the long-haul network can be enormous, and the supply of stand-by aircraft is far from infinite. An aircraft which goes out of commission for technical reasons in Delhi on its way home to London should be operating a service out of Heathrow the following day. Operations' job is not only to sort out the problem down the route, but to plug the gap which is about to appear at home base. The airline gives them a free hand – to cancel flights if necessary, to charter in other airlines' aircraft to pick up BA passengers who would otherwise be stranded. 'As a result,' says the ops manager, 'we are not necessarily always the most popular people around.' Between 3 and 5 am each day, engineering produces a report on the state of readiness of the fleet for the following day, so that ops can finalise the programme at crack of dawn. This is the final sharp end of a plan which has begun life five years earlier, when the airline's planning department has gazed into the distant future to determine what routes are to be flown, what airliners will be needed to operate them, how many pilots and cabin staff will be required to man the aircraft, and how many staff need to be recruited to back up the whole operation.

Contact with all BA's stations and airliners is maintained through an awesome array of high-technology communications systems embracing computers, telex, the telephone, and single sideband radio over a company channel. Using the latter, ops control is able to speak directly to the crew of BA aircraft wherever they are, whether flying or on the ground, to listen to their problems, suggest solutions, or order diversions. BA engineers sit in at the ops room. If one of the systems of a distant aircraft is playing up, they can tell the pilots and flight engineer how important – or otherwise – the snag is and, if a diversion of the flight is necessary, which alternate station along the route holds replacement parts. BA keeps its own engineers at all of the bigger points on its world-wide network, and they generally pop in to the Heathrow ops room when home on leave to put faces to the distant voices they talk with over the lines to their far-flung corners of the universe. As one of them commented, on one such visit, 'I'm glad there is somebody to hold my hand at three o'clock in the morning.'

Twelve noon, and the British Airways big birds are leaving the roost in numbers for exotic spots a world away, to the accompaniment of loud-speaker announcements which make places like the Seychelles, Mauritius, Sydney and San Francisco sound routine – which, for Terminal 4, they are. The jumbos and the TriStars which touched down at Heathrow in the early hours of this same morning are now refuelled, revictualled (the airline serves its passengers some 26 million meals in flight each year), engineered, cleaned, and loaded with cargo (nearly half a million tonnes shifted during the 1988–9 fiscal, worth almost £1 million a day in revenue), and are ready to go again. The key figure in the run-up to the departure of every flight is the aircraft despatcher, one of a brigade of 200 in the airline, identifiable by their red caps, who appears an hour and a half before the flight is due to push back from the gate, and who has to be in peak fitness as he, or she, will on average dash up and down the steep service ladder which connects the main deck of a 747 with the ground 35 feet below anything up to fifteen times during that period.

'We will', says one of them, 'do almost anything to make sure that our aircraft leaves on time, safely and correctly loaded,' adding, 'but there are days where everything seems to try to conspire to stop you from doing that.' The despatcher keeps what is literally a running check on what is happening on the apron beneath the airliner, where up to thirty service vehicles come and go, in the aircraft itself, and in the final departure lounge, where the passengers are assembling. He notes that the engineers have completed their checks, that the correct number of meals for the number of passengers have been delivered (including any special requests for vegetarian or relig-ious diets), that the cargo is being loaded on time, that the passengers' baggage is coming forward for stowing, that the refuelling trucks are present and are delivering the correct amount of fuel (the 747 will burn off 600 kilos just taxiing out to the end of the runway).

Life then becomes departure minus so many minutes, and the action begins to speed up like a film shown at the wrong speed. Minus 55 minutes, and a bus arrives at the foot of the steps carrying the cabin crew, who scatter throughout the jumbo's interior, checking their supplies and giving the cabin a final primp. Minus 45 minutes, and another transport draws up, this time bearing the captain, co-pilot and flight engineer. Both groups are briefed by the despatcher on the progress towards departure, and are warned of any problems which have shown themselves and which may lead to a delay.

Minus 35, and the despatcher is back at the departure lounge, for by then the passengers are being asked to go on board. There are the inevitable queries at the desks as boarding cards and tickets are checked. Some passengers are transferring to the flight from another, but the lounge is now empty and there is still no sign of them. The Red Cap's walkie-talkie radio crackles and he announces that they are on their way. This statement is confirmed a few seconds later by the sound of running feet in the corridor; the missing persons – 'have-a-goes' as they are known in airline language (because they are sent off to 'have-a-go' to reach the flight before the doors are closed) – appear at the lounge door, flustered and out of breath, to be smoothed down the air bridge and on to the aircraft.

After that, it is back at sprinter's pace now to the 747 and, at minus 10 minutes, up the staircase which connects its main passenger floor with the upper deck and cockpit (another 15-foot climb) to hand the captain the load sheet, an essential document which has been drawn up by the Aircraft Despatch Department. As its name indicates, the load sheet details everything that the aircraft is carrying, from passengers to fuel, from baggage to cargo, their weights, and the manner in which the load is distributed around the aircraft. By way of the load sheet, the centre of gravity of the airliner has been established precisely – vital if it is to take off smoothly, and at the correct point down the runway, and to fly 'cleanly' once it is cruising, so reducing the amount of fuel which it uses.

Minus 8 minutes, and the tempo is now really fast. The powerful tractor tug, built low to slide beneath the airliner's belly and with wheels almost as high as the tractor is tall, is summoned over the radio to push the jumbo back from its stand. Minus 5, and the Red Cap is down the ladder once more to make sure that all the hold doors are securely closed. Then back to the end of the air bridge for a final cheery farewell to the cabin staff as they swing the main passenger door to and thump it into position. With the air jetty driven away, the despatcher returns to the apron for the last time, for the moment towards which he has been working over the past hour and a half. The tractor moves into gear, and this leviathan of the skies, lights flashing, attendant ground staff walking beneath each wing to see her clear, moves somewhat ignominiously backwards at the start of a journey which is to take it half-way around the world.

Not all departures go so smoothly. In the atmosphere of heightened security, the one thing no airline will do today is to despatch a service with a passenger whose name is on the manifest not on board, and with his or her bags loaded. In such a case, with everybody and everything else ready to roll, and with the take-off slot allocated for the flight becoming nail-bitingly near, a search starts for the absentee. But the problem with finding an individual in Terminal 4 is that it is a vast facility. Opened in the spring of 1986 by the Prince and Princess of Wales, it was twelve years in the planning, development and building phase, cost £200 million, and is designed to handle eight million-plus passengers a year. The departures concourse is 650 metres long and 25 metres wide, with flights boarded from seventeen different gates. Unlike most other airports, passengers are not marshalled in individual gate-rooms before going on board but are free to wander until their service is called over the public address system.

Usually, therefore, missing passengers are not really missing, but are at the far end of the concourse, engrossed in the duty-free and tax-free shops, still in the bar, or have fallen asleep. Although there are probably 350 travellers on the waiting flight, amazingly enough the check-in staff can usually recall at least a rough idea of what the absentee looks like, or what clothes he or she is wearing. BA staff go off hunting the quarry. Normally they are tracked down quickly, to be hurried aboard to endure the stares and glares of the other 349. But when the absentee cannot be traced, the airline has a big problem, and the departure time of the flight will be put off for anything up to two hours while the holds are opened up and every one of the bags in them – and on the basis that each long-haul passenger travels with an average of 1.5, there will be 525 individual pieces – will be examined to find those belonging to the missing passenger. Only when these are removed, to be taken away for examination by the airport bomb squad, will the flight be allowed to go.

The pattern of arrivals and departures is repeated as the day goes by. A further Concorde flight departs for Washington and Miami at 4.25 pm every other afternoon, the 003 Concorde for New York every day at 6.45 pm; with the five-hour time difference between London and the east coast of the United States, both will arrive at an earlier local time than that at which they departed Heathrow. The last BA departure of the day is the long-haul down to Rio, which pushes back at 10.25 pm; the last arrival is the 004 Concorde from New York, whose passengers decant into a, by now, almost deserted Terminal 4 shortly after 10.30 pm. By that time BA will have coped during that working day with around 10 400 inbound passengers and about 10 600 outbound, plus their 30 000 bags. Terminal 4 then draws breath for a few short hours: the cleaners dust and polish, the restaurants and snack bars are restocked, BA's night staff pore over the results of the day just gone and the forecasts for that ahead. And at 5 am the 747 from Seoul, Tokyo and Anchorage touches down on runway 28 Left and it all begins again.

CHAPTER TWO

MERGER AND SURVIVAL

To trace the history of British Airways, it is necessary to go back seventy years to a field at Hounslow, Middlesex, near the airline's present base at Heathrow. There at 9.10 in the morning of 25 August 1919, Aircraft Transport and Travel Ltd (AT&T) launched an air service to Paris Le Bourget. The aircraft was a de Havilland Airco 4A, a wooden-framed, wire-braced, canvas-covered biplane, originally designed as a bomber for the recently-ended war. Registration G-EAJC, it was powered by a Rolls-Royce Eagle VI engine developing 360 hp, and had a top speed of 121 mph. Its pilot was Lieutenant Bill Lawford AFC, whose habit was to call everyone, from senior management downwards, 'old man'.

Two hours and 20 minutes after leaving London, the flight landed safely at Paris, Lawford having navigated his way by compass and by peering over the side for the names of railway stations, painted in white letters on their roofs. Flying by Bradshaw, as it was known.

With the war so recently over there were hundreds of ex-bomber aircraft going for a song and legions of demobilised pilots anxious to fly them. Many of the new airlines which sprang up soon ran into financial trouble and their services did not last long. By early 1921 all scheduled British air services had ceased. Britain's new premier airport at Croydon was, for a short time, used only by foreign airlines.

The British government of the day weighed in with subsidies of £75 000 to help four of the British airlines re-establish themselves, but by the end of 1923 these four small companies were merged into Imperial Air Transport – which became, the following year, Imperial Airways.

Imperial opened services to Paris in 1924, but it had its eyes on points beyond Europe and plans were soon laid for links to be opened with the British Empire. The first through service to India left Croydon in 1929; the Cape, in South Africa, was reached two years later.

Flagship of the Imperial fleet during the 1930s on both the European and long-distance routes was the Handley Page HP 42 airliner, a veritable galleon of the skies, with four Bristol Jupiter engines, big biplane wings, and a triple-finned biplane tail. Between 1931 and the outbreak of war in 1939, Imperial's eight airliners of this type flew over ten million miles between them without hurting a hair on the head of a single passenger. Absolute top speed was measured as 136 mph, and the story goes that, as one of them was rumbling majestically across Europe, the captain, who was exchanging pleasantries with the passengers in one of the cabins, was approached with due deference by the steward. 'Excuse me, sir,' said the latter. 'First officer sends his compliments and asks that you might return to the cockpit. There's an Alp coming up.'

Public interest in the burgeoning airlines was enormous, and was fuelled still further by the opportunity which the industry presented to speed letters from one end of the globe to the other. The Empire Air Mail Scheme, introduced in late 1934, caught the public imagination and produced for Imperial the startling total of 2000 tons of mail a year. To carry it, the airline made the brave move of ordering, straight from the drawing-board, twenty-eight Short 'C', or 'Empire' class, flying boats. Before long this fleet was taking over the routes to Australia and South Africa. Imperial's next step was to span the North Atlantic, but experiments in mail-carrying and in-flight refuelling were brought to a halt by the outbreak of war.

The faltering progress being made by the civil aviation industry in the 1930s was speeded up through the multi-billions which were poured into it by way of the war budgets. Britain entered the war with the 130-mph HP 42 as a flagship airliner; she emerged six yeas later with an operational jet fighter. In the confusion of the opening weeks of World War 2, the formation of British Overseas Airways Corporation (BOAC) on 24 November 1939, out of a merger betweeen Imperial Airways and the former British Airways, went virtually unnoticed. During the war the fledgling BOAC flew a number of operations which had more to do with cloak-and-dagger than with airline services, but which kept vital lifelines open.

As had happened after the First World War, the first post-war airliners were converted bombers. BOAC used Lancastrians, based on the Lancaster bomber, to fly between Hurn, near Bournemouth, and Sydney, Australia, and Haltons, based on the Halifax, to serve West Africa. Post-war civil aviation in Britain was formalised by the Civil Aviation Act of 1946, which established British South American Airways (it was merged with BOAC in 1949) and British European Airways. BEA started up on 4 February that year as a division of BOAC, and was established in its own right on 1 August. Its earliest aircraft were ex-RAF DC-3 Dakotas, some still in their wartime camouflage, while its first pilots wore their RAF uniforms in the absence of anything else. Its main base was the RAF station at Northolt, a few miles to the north of the present London Heathrow airport.

By 1950 peacetime aviation was beginning to find its stride again, with both BOAC and BEA investing in aircraft specially designed for civil flying rather than converted from military types. BOAC bought Constellations, Argonauts, Stratocruisers and Hermes; BEA acquired Ambassadors and the turboprop Viscount, using the former (which it renamed the Elizabethan) to reopen the Silver Wing service between London and Paris.

BOAC became the first airline in the world to enter the jet era when, on 2 May 1952, a de Havilland Comet 1 in its colours left Heathrow, into which the airlines had moved the previous year, for Johannesburg. Two years later both the airline and the manufacturer paid the penalty suffered by many pioneers. The story of the crash of a Comet off Elba, followed by a similiar disaster off Naples soon after, the withdrawal of the certificate of airworthiness, and the painstaking investigation into what went wrong, is well enough known not to be repeated here. In the four years that it took to develop a strengthened Comet 4, the Americans came along with their Boeing 707s, which BOAC subsequently bought, and Douglas DC-8s, so that Britain's initial lead was wasted away.

BEA, too, bought Comet 4s, followed by a fleet of Tridents. BOAC invested in the VC 10, and then, as the era of mass air travel began in the early 1970s, in the Boeing 747 'jumbo jets'. With Air France the airline ushered in the supersonic era. On 21 January 1976, it opened its Concorde service to Bahrain, while AF flew to Rio de Janeiro. In the space of fifty-seven years, from that first tentative service between London and Paris, the speed of British commercial aviation had risen from 121 to 1350 mph, or 2.2 times the speed of sound.

A merger of BEA and BOAC was ordered by the British government in the early 1970s in the interests of efficiency, but this was not an attribute which came easily to the new British Airways when it was established under its first chairman, Sir David Nicolson. The problems of pulling two such totally different companies together were enormous. Both BEA and BOAC were in the business of flying aeroplanes, but the similarity ceased there; management structure and style, and route networks, were totally different. There was an opinion within BEA that the people at BOAC were *dilettantes*, to whom such outside forces as fuel crises, or the business of getting airliners away on time, were of little concern, a gentleman's airline with roots still embedded in the leisurely pre-war days of Imperial, even an extension of the Foreign Office. Conversely, there were those in BOAC who looked down upon BEA, with its largely ex-Service management, as a tradesman's outfit, its short-haul routes bringing it scuttling back to base each day.

The opening years of the merger were spent in attempts to pull these two disparate sides together against an unhappy background of in-fighting between the managements of the merged airlines – which included the smaller domestic carrier British Air Services (BAS). For the majority of the executive directorships in the new BA there were three contenders, from BEA, from BOAC, and from BAS, and it was not always necessarily the best man, or the most senior, or the most experienced, who was selected. Personal animosities played a role. Walk-outs after decades of service in the airlines were not unknown. Curiously, the old British practice of 'Buggins' turn', under which the chap who didn't get the job this time can be fairly certain of being favoured next time round, did not play a major part in the process, and it was largely fortuitous that the final shape was reasonably well balanced between BEA and BOAC (although old BOAC men will still tell you that BEA men took the plum jobs, and vice versa). Meanwhile the merged airline, moving towards a peak of 58 000 employees, was wallowing along on a day-to-day operating basis, but this was a time of boom for the industry and nobody was too worried that productivity was low. The new British Airways, it was thought, would grow comfortably into the overlarge new coat which it had assumed. Sir Frank McFadzean (later Lord McFadzean), who took over the chairmanship of BA in 1976 after a lengthy career running Shell, began to take a grip on the productivity issue. He also fought and won a brisk battle with the government of the day on the question of new short-haul aircraft to replace the ageing and thirsty Trident fleet. The contenders were the British BAC 1-11 and the American Boeing 737. On its track record the British flag-carrying airline would have gone for the British product, but in the opinion of the BA planners the US-made aeroplane was the more efficient, and the 737 was ordered.

With the appearance on the airline scene in the late 1970s of Freddie Laker with his concept of cheap air travel, the BA management identified the new breed of airline typified by Laker Airways, with its high productivity and low costs, as the biggest competitive challenge for the future, rather than the traditional airlines like Lufthansa and Air France.

Roy Watts, who had joined BEA in 1955, progressing to chairman and chief executive and then becoming BA chief executive (1979–82) and deputy chairman and group MD (1982–3), was charged in 1978 with producing a board paper, 'Airline Scenario 1986', laying down a strategic policy which would take the airline at least into the middle of the next decade. Viewed with the benefit of hindsight today, most of the paper can be seen as a remarkably accurate exercise in crystal-ball gazing. For instance, the use of conference videophones would not oust business travel; work on a Channel rail tunnel would begin; there would be an increase in long-haul competition from other carriers; there would be airport, runway and air traffic control (ATC) congestion. BA, the paper urged, should concentrate on all segments of the market – 'the only viable option' – with judgement of the extent of participation in the low-yield market being crucial in determining the long-term profitability of the airline. Staff productivity would increase so that the airline would have the same number of employees in 1986 as in 1978. 'High productivity is an essential element of competitive cost levels,' the paper stated. 'Achievement is probably BA's most difficult task.' The main conclusion was that to compete with the 'Laker syndrome' BA would have to lower its overall costs by 15%, or some £300 million, on a yearly basis.

As the merger, which in the words of one close observer had been both 'a long, tedious process' and 'a thoroughly bloody affair', finally came together in the late 1970s, innovation was certainly not unknown. Under the direction of Roy Watts, British Airways introduced the concept of the shuttle on the London–Glasgow trunk route in 1975, extending to Edinburgh the following year, Belfast in 1977, and Manchester in 1979. BA managers had been to New York to investigate the then Eastern Airlines shuttle operation between La Guardia and Washington National. Many of the EA ideas were grafted on to the BA shuttle, particularly the guarantee to carry everybody who turned up for a flight, even if an extra aircraft had to be whistled up for one passenger, and pay-on-board, with cabin staff collecting the fares as the flight progressed. This latter concept resulted in an industrial dispute over which group of BA staff should sell tickets. The dispute was one of a number which disrupted the airline during this period, playing hell with its punctuality performance and its image with the travelling public. Engineers and baggage-loaders were two particularly militant groups, and the sight of management humping luggage and driving baggage carts on the ramp became commonplace. BA management had inherited 2000 shop stewards among its 35 000 employees at its main base at Heathrow, plus a series of running battles in which concessions were expected if the airline was to keep flying.

This was before legislation curbing the power of the trade unions had been passed by Parliament, and well before the days, later on in the 1980s, when there were three million out of work. The most significant thing which BA's management accomplished towards the happier state which exists today between it and the trade unions was the establishing, in the late 1970s, of BATUC, the British Airways Trade Union Council, at whose monthly meetings representatives of the airline's trade unions met across the table with the airline's executive directors. No negotiating or bargaining points were allowed (in fact, the TU representatives were quick to blanket colleagues who wanted to start negotiations). Meetings were a frank exchange of views, and the BA side took the trade unions completely into their confidence on financial and economic matters. It was a *rapport* which paid great dividends when the economic bottom suddenly dropped out of the world marketplace, the airline industry in general, and BA in particular, as the 1980s began.

As early as September 1980 Roy Watts wrote to staff, warning them of an impending 'very serious' situation and listing remedial measures, but at the beginning of April the following year the downturn became a roller-coaster. Everybody hoped that the trend would be short-lived, but as the summer progressed it became increasingly obvious that there was to be no quick bottoming-out. BA began to lose money, it was estimated, at the rate of nearly £200 every minute, and it was rapidly borne in upon those running the airline that unless something very drastic was done the airline would bleed to financial death.

Watts considered the situation deeply in the lengthy thinking time afforded by a journey back from Papua New Guinea, and when he landed at Heathrow on a Sunday night in early September what was to become known as the British Airways Survival Plan had already crystallised in his mind. First thing on the Monday morning, the executive directors were called in and told to produce a programme of sweeping cuts. There was no argument about it; it was made clear that the very existence of BA was at stake. Speed was vital. The work to flesh out the survival plan went on throughout the following days, occasionally through the night, under conditions of great secrecy. By the Friday it was complete and Watts took it to his board, by that time headed by Sir John King, who had succeeded Sir Ross Stainton as chairman the previous February. The board agreed it virtually on the nod, as did BATUC. The first that the public, and the great majority of BA's employees, knew of it was when a special staff bulletin, printed by a security printer which specialised in work for the Ministry of Defence, came out with big headlines, 'Tough Measures For Survival' and 'Routes, Stations, Bases, Staff, Aircraft To Go'.

The headlines were alarming, but were an understatement. The survival plan was swingeing in its breadth and scope, even brutal; no sentiment was allowed to intrude, no sacred cows allowed to remain. Reducing staff numbers was the major priority; these had begun to come down from the peak of 58 000 in September 1979, and with the impetus of the survival plan touched a low of 37 000 by February 1983. The plan placed an immediate bar on all recruiting – when people left they were not replaced – so saving some 4000 positions a year. In the language of the high street, 'almost everything had to go'. Sixteen international passenger routes out of Heathrow, Gatwick or regional airports, which were losing money and which showed no sign of coming good, were closed down. Concorde services to Singapore, which were losing £7 million a year for BA and Singapore Airlines, were cancelled. A question mark was raised over the future of the highlands and islands network in Scotland. Eight stations were earmarked for closure by the following spring – Prestwick, Luxembourg, Belgrade, Zagreb, Sofia, Bucharest, Salonica and Valencia. Engineering bases at Manchester and Cardiff were to go.

Sixteen aircraft were put up for sale or lease, inluding the whole of the all-cargo fleet, consisting of one Boeing 747F and three 707s. All freight was in future to be carried in the belly holds of passenger aircraft. Two passenger 707s were to be moved off the inventory as were seven Trident 2s. Two Boeing 747s built but not delivered were cancelled, but the new fleet of Boeing 757s which had been ordered was left untouched, saved by the promise of low fuel and operating costs. Six TriStars were sold to the RAF for conversion to troop-carriers and aerial tankers at what was generally considered in the industry to be a knock-down price of some £10 million each. As part of the survival plan, a survey of properties occupied by BA had turned up a remarkable collection. The rapid fall-off in staff numbers had left acres of office space unoccupied, and once again the axe was swung energetically. Both BEA's and BOAC's spiritual homes, Bealine House, built as a school on the edge of Northolt aerodrome, and the Victoria Air Terminal in the heart of London, from where Imperial Airways journeys used to start, were among the properties put on the market. The airline's staff college, at East Burnham, Buckinghamshire, was closed down and offered for sale, as was the College of Air Training, at Hamble, Southampton, on the assumption that BA would not be requiring any new pilots for a very long time. Staff sports and social clubs came up for the chop – this producing the only deputation from staff to management in the whole affair when the sports club asked Roy Watts for a reprieve, pointing out that he used the facilities to play squash; they received a dusty answer. One activity which did survive was the engineering apprentice school, largely because it had recently won a valuable contract to train airline apprentices from overseas. But there was no new intake of BA engineering apprentices, nor any other type of trainee, that year.

At Heathrow, the northside catering centre was transferred from an in-house operation to an outside catering firm, as was all staff catering at the airline's main base. It was a trend which was to permeate the whole airline, management realising that there were a lot of expensive specialist activities which could be handed over to third parties. Widespread cuts were ordered in administrative services like typing pools, copying centres, communications, postal services, and computer and consultancy activities. It was made clear to the staff that consideration of pay increases was out of the question before September 1982 at the earliest, that there would be no increase in shift pay or London weighting (extra allowance to meet the higher cost of working in the London area), and that ways of reducing the cost to BA of staff pensions, which were then costing the airline over £67 million a year, would be negotiated. Volunteers were sought who were willing to leave the airline at short notice – compulsory redundancy, the staff was told, would not be introduced 'if it can be helped'. The terms ranged from 50% of one year's pensionable pay for those with less than three years' service, to 150% for those with fifteen years and over.

It was a formidable package, and the surprising fact was that it went through, to form the launch platform for BA's success in the mid-1980s, with virtually no protest from the airline's staff, despite their having to watch their company taken apart, heavily massaged, and put back together again in a radically different form. The worst backlash against the reform came from baggage-loaders in Terminal 1 at Heathrow, where the scaling down in the number of jobs had hit particularly hard, and where management were seeking to streamline union practices. They went on strike for eight weeks in the spring of 1982, but the airline was run without them, with employees from other trades, from pilots to check-in staff, helping to load and unload the luggage. The story goes inside the airline that that baggage system worked so smoothly during the period of the dispute that it provoked a puzzled message from one of the Norwegian stations asking what was going on. Were the monthly baggage-loss figures, normally so dismal, incorrect?

One of the main reasons for the general acceptance of the survival plan by staff was that, immediately it was made public, communication channels between staff and management had been opened wide. Those channels had been utilised by Roy Watts to leave nobody on the payroll in any doubt whatsoever of the extreme seriousness of the situation in which the airline found itself. His message was blunt. He told them that British Airways was facing the worst crisis in its history, and that unless swift and drastic remedies were taken, the airline would lose at least £100 million in the current financial year, and a total of £250 million by April 1982. No business, he said, could survive losses on this scale, and there was a real possibility that British Airways would go out of business for a lack of money. 'We have to cut our costs sharply, and we have to cut them fast. We have no more choice, and no more time,' he wrote to the staff. The rescue measures had to be taken swiftly, because the time to debate them at leisure could no longer be afforded.

The measures were tough, Watts went on, but they were not panic measures, and nothing would be done which would undermine the strength of the fleet, the international and national routes, and the airline's technical and commercial resources. A fundamental element of the rescue plan was to reduce manpower costs quickly and substantially. However good BA was technically, it would not be able to exist in the increasingly competitive future unless it reduced cost levels. 'The plain truth is that during the years of rapid growth, and particularly after the merger, British Airways grew fat. As a result, staff costs are now our biggest single bill at nearly £700 million a year. We have to reduce that by at least £100 million a year if we are to survive. The stark choice now is between offering a lot fewer jobs, or offering no jobs at all. There are no other courses left to us.' Unless these steps were taken, there was no prospect of a return to prosperity, Roy Watts said, ending with the warning, 'And until we do, there can be no real job security for any of us.'

By the summer of 1982 the survival plan was beginning to bite, but keeping up the momentum towards becoming a lean airline was not easy, and there were continuing management exhortations to staff to do better. By that time the airline had been re-formed into three operating divisions: Intercontinental, European and Gatwick. One senior manager laid it on the line bluntly: 'I believe our new organisation gives British Airways the best chance it has ever had to become a highly efficient commercial airline. I hope I'm right, because it's not only our best chance, but probably our last chance too.'

To give a flavour of the new set-up, European Services Division had ninety aircraft operating over ninety routes in Europe and Britain, carrying ten million passengers a year on some 2000 scheduled services a week. The plan was that it should operate largely as an independent airline, with the support of a central organisation which flew and maintained the aircraft, handled passengers at Heathrow, and provided administrative services like personnel and revenue accounting. By 1982, European Services Division management told staff, punctuality had improved, 'fit to rate with the best', from a position two years earlier when it was 'a disgrace'. Management sought to drive home the message that BA was not in business just to fly the flag, or to run a social service, or to provide work for the aircraft factories. The airline was there to make a profit by providing something that people wanted to buy – just like any other business. BA, staff were assured, had to make an adequate profit, or it would be asked to move over and let somebody else do it.

There was, in fact, in BA at that time a very real apprehension that under the Thatcher government, with its accent away from mollycoddling by the state and in favour of thrusting free enterprise, at least part of BA's role of national flag-carrier could be handed over to the independent sector in Britain if the airline did not save itself by its own financial efforts. There was the precedent of another famous household British name going bust – Rolls-Royce in 1971 – with another Tory government proclaiming the ethos that it would not save lame ducks. In that instance it was quickly borne in upon government that if there were no Rolls-Royce, a quarter of the world's airlines and air forces would be quickly grounded for lack of spare parts for their Rolls-Royce engines, and so a bailing-out operation was put in hand. But whereas there had been no substitute for Rolls-Royce, there were plenty of other airlines which could come in to compete with a lame BA. Such fears undoubtedly provided a spur to the efforts of both management and staff to shed BA's surplus weight. In the light of government preparedness a few years later to write off £500 million of BA's indebtedness as a way of preparing the airline for privatisation, the fears were probably unfounded, but they were certainly current in the early 1980s and they helped to propel BA along its flight path towards recovery.

By mid-1982 BA was still struggling to achieve this aim. European Division's revenue during that financial year was going to be close on £700 million, and its target was a surplus of £50 million over that. But, employees were warned by the time the division had repaid its share of the money that BA had borrowed to buy aircraft, the net profit would be a mere £17 million – not nearly enough to set aside for new aircraft for the future. 'Potential rivals are eagerly breathing down our necks, keen to get on some of our most-important routes,' the workers were warned. Big increases in revenue were needed, but this was a period when European air fares were beginning to show a downward trend. The answer was to be better control of yield, and of the pro-rates (the share of the overall fare passed on to other airlines when two or more carriers were involved in a journey). It did not mean getting into profitless, under-the-counter fares wars for the sake of obtaining a few more cut-price customers, 'who can't be carried profitably anyway'.

Although there had been sweeping route cuts the year before, BA management were identifying in 1982 a lot more which were a dead loss – routes which not only did not earn their keep, but which drained money from the more profitable ones. Something like half the routes in European Division were, in fact, losing money. Management warned again, 'If anything happens to that handful of profitable routes, like a sudden drop in business, or an international crisis, or the kind of competition that produced a fares war like we've seen on the North Atlantic, then this division would sink like a stone.' But, staff were assured, the airline was not in the business of closing routes, except as an absolute last resort. What was wanted was to cure them, get them back into profit, not kill them.

By this time the airline had made considerable strides towards increased productivity, both on the ground and in the air, with the worldwide staff reduced by 16 000, or around 30%. But despite this, as BA's management knew from studying other airlines, BA was still using a lot more people than its most efficient competitors to achieve a comparable level of output. An exhortation to staff of that time read:

> We know there's a strong feeling that every time we want to save money, we cut down on the number of people who actually do the work and who look after our customers, and that we don't take the axe to the back-room bureaucracy. We're keeping a very tight watch on our own divisional costs, and we've made sure that our head office is a very lean organisation.

More work was required from the airliners, as well as from the employees, who were told that if utilisation could be raised by 120 hours a year for each aircraft in the European fleet, that would save the equivalent of three or four aircraft.

Admonition such as this, plus the deep cuts inherent in the plan for survival, and some innovatory ideas for attracting more high-yield passengers, slowly and painfully dragged British Airways back on course. During the early 1980s the airline looked to its 'product', began to cosset its fare-paying passengers, brushed up its punctuality, lost less of its customers' luggage. A manager of the old school, who said of a long-haul service standing at Heathrow waiting to go, 'You can either have the cargo loaded, or you can have a punctual departure,' was told in no uncertain terms that from that day on the airline would have both. An operations director, Howard Phelps, was appointed, with a seat on the executive board and the power to probe into reasons for late departures – he even had one of the airline's video-display screens, showing the up-to-the-minute state of the network, installed in his living-room at home.

The all-important yield began to rise through the introduction by Roy Watts during the 1980–1 period of what was known at that time as 'the new European product'. This involved the sweeping away of the first-class cabin on all European routes as a big money-loser, and its replacement with club class, now Club Europe. Serious doubts were expressed within the airline as to the wisdom of this move, but its rightness was soon proved on two counts. Firstly, the majority of the other major European airlines followed suit – today only Lufthansa and Swissair fly European routes with first-class cabins. Secondly, BA quickly captured 33% of its traffic between Britain and Europe in its premium-fare, club-class cabins, utilising a movable divider to stretch or shorten those cabins at short notice before a flight was due to depart. One innovatory idea which did not succeed was to spread the shuttle concept from the UK domestic routes to the trunk routes between Heathrow and the continent – Paris, Amsterdam and Brussels. BA pushed it, but the national airlines of the continental countries would not follow through, on grounds that they might lose their national identities.

Sleeperseats, super club class, and segregated check-in were introduced for the intercontinental services from 1981. Slowly BA lost its fat, dumb and happy image. Three years after the plan for survival was sprung, it could boast that departures within fifteen minutes of schedule on its intercontinental services were 74%, an improvement of 110% on 1979–80, and on European services 80%, an improvement of 25% over the same period. Shuttle departures within fifteen minutes were running at over 90%. Regularity of service had been improved dramatically, with 99.5% of planned operations actually performed. Claims for lost and damaged baggage were being settled at a rate of two per thousand passengers, an improvement of 22% since 1979–80. Passenger complaints were 2.1 per thousand passengers, a reduction of 19% since 1979–80 and 11% since 1981–2. Between the 1980–1 and the 1983–4 financial years, airline capacity in terms of available tonne kilometres (ATKs) had gone down

14%, the seat factor (the percentage of seats on offer which were actually sold) went up 5.3 points, and the overall load factor (seats and cargo) by 5.2 points.

Utilisation of the aircraft fleet, measured in the annual average hours flown per aircraft, was 2522 in 1979–80, 2359 in 1980–1, 2287 in 1981–2, 2535 in 1982–3 and 2667 in 1983–4, an overall increase of 13.1%, or 4.2% per year. Staff productivity, measured in units of production per staff, went up between 1980–1 and 1983–4 by 36%, or 10.8% per year, while the total cost of staff pay, pensions and insurance reduced by 13%, or 33% in real terms. Most importantly of all, the airline's cost per unit of production had reduced by 22%, or 7.8% per year, in terms of staff pay, and by 7%, or 2.3% per year, covering all costs. And by reducing staff numbers to 37 000, BA had just about measured up to the traditional yardstick of efficiency applied by the airlines in the United States – that you should be able to carry all of your staff in your aircraft fleet, without any left over. The severance costs for the 20 000 who had gone were expensive (£199 million was allotted in the 1981–2 accounts) but were one-time payments. The annual savings of £300 million were there to be savoured for years ahead.

With the arrival of Sir John (later Lord) King as chairman in early 1981, Gordon Dunlop as financial director in June 1982, and Colin Marshall as chief executive in February 1983, British Airways closed a chapter in its existence and embarked on a new era. None of them had any background in the airline industry, nor were they impressed by the mystique of the aviation business. Each had lengthy experience of commercial affairs in the world outside the airways and the airports, and each arrived determined to apply that experience towards the completion of BA's financial and economic turnaround, and to preparing the company – the overriding brief – for the switch from the public to the private sector. Like-minded businessmen were invited in from outside to assist them in this task. Many of the old professional airline men who had soldiered on from the BOAC and BEA days were, often abruptly, told that their services were no longer required, while others elected to take early retirement. Such fundamental changes in management structure were not effected without some deep personal pain. Not all the airline's pros went, however; some rose to the top during the upheaval, a case in point being Jim Harris, a BOAC man since leaving grammar school in 1946, who was appointed marketing director responsible for the airline's worldwide marketing policy soon after Colin Marshall arrived. When Harris finally retired in spring 1989, to be succeeded by Liam Strong, another of the new generation of executives from commerce outside the airlines, he had been with the airline for forty-three years and was given an affectionate public send-off by Lord King.

But Harris and a few of his old BOAC and BEA colleagues apart, most of the airline men who survived the 'nights of the long knives' were young, or youngish. A radical reorganisation of the management structure unveiled in the summer of 1983 promoted twelve potential high-fliers, half of them in their thirties. The reorganisation swept away the existing three service divisions and replaced them with eight market centres, and three business centres, covering cargo, charters and tours. Colin Marshall said, 'This new organisation makes it possible for us to move quickly to respond to customer needs in any area of the world.' And in a nod in the direction of those who were going out as the new men came in through the revolving doors, he added, 'We could never have reached this point of success so soon had it not been for the efforts of some of the senior executives who are now retiring or leaving us.' The stamina of youth was certainly an asset in those early days of the new BA management. Gone was any suggestion of a cosy nine-to-five existence, with weekends off as a matter of course. Colin Marshall was usually in his office by 7 am, or down in the departure lounge seeing off the first shuttle service of the day, during which excursions he would go on board the aircraft to make sure that the cabins were well dressed for the flight, and then solicit opinions about the service from passengers waiting to board. Routine meetings were called at 7.30 am or 7 pm. Lights in individual offices in the Speedbird House headquarters burned late into the evening. Sunday afternoon conferences were not unknown.

As an aside, but an indication of what Marshall had called 'moving quickly to respond to customer needs', shuttle went through a radical change of product in August 1983, becoming Super Shuttle and beginning to serve food and drinks on board. BA management had been stung into action by the increasingly tough competition on the shuttle routes from Michael Bishop's British Midland Airways, which was giving on-board service and was eating into BA's market share. And although shuttle was a high-cost operation, with a high proportion of resources thrown into it to maintain the promise of a seat for everybody, by the summer of 1983 it was carrying 2½ million passengers a year, or one-seventh of all the passengers the airline flew worldwide.

The London *Standard* had said that June:

Competition really is good for us consumers . . . British Midland Airways has smashed British Airways' domination of our domestic air routes, and freed us from their hateful shuttle service . . . After only six months, BMA has captured a third of the London–Glasgow passengers, and a quarter of the London–Edinburgh market . . . Meals and drinks appropriate to the time of day are included in the fare, unlike the BA no-frills, we'll-take-less-care-of-you service. BA admits that its shuttle service is more expensive to run because it guarantees a back-up plane if the first plane is full, and it says this guarantee provides it with extra passengers. So why has a chunk of its market just switched to a rival service?

And a letter in *Flight International* at around the same time had also made some wounding points:

> The Trident [shuttle] service operated by BA has a cabin crew of three. On a 70-min. flight, some 10 min. is spent seated for take-off and landing. Of the remaining 60 min., 15 min. is spent collecting fares, while the remaining 45 min. are spent behind the curtains, knitting, reading, etc. By simply calculating their productivity as working time (15 min.) over available working time (60 min.) one arrives at a productivity of 25%. The productivity on BMA flights, calculated on the same basis, is a staggering 83% (and that is a minimum). On its DC-9 flights, using the same number of cabin crew, i.e. three, they are working for at least 50 min. of the same 60 min. available time. During the flight one is provided with a sweet before take-off and landing, refreshments from a drinks trolley, and a meals service ranging from a full dinner with wine, to tea/coffee and biscuits, depending upon time of day. If this productivity difference is reflected in other parts of the airline's operation, then BA still has a long way to go.

There was no time for knitting and reading in the King/Marshall New Model Airline. The changes in work practices which were introduced into shuttle were reflected right round the airline, both on the ground and in the air. Colin Marshall set out to restore not only public confidence, but also the morale of the staff, badly bruised during the traumas which they had so recently been through, the financial crises, the redundancies, the changes in management and management style. His business antecedents fitted him perfectly for the task, for most of his career had been with companies with a high public profile, and in which the staff were constantly motivated to do better than the opposition. 'We Try Harder' had been the motto of the American Avis car hire company, which he joined in 1964, rising to chairman of the board before he left in 1981 to join Sears Holdings, the British high street shops conglomerate which has Selfridges as its flagship, as a director and deputy chief executive. Marshall was taken on by Avis to develop the company's car hire business in Europe, a brief which he accomplished with signal success: when he arrived, Avis had six cars for hire in London; on his departure, the total in Britain was 14 000 cars and vans. Before Avis he was with the rival Hertz from 1958 to 1964, starting off helping to clean returned cars on the forecourt, and ending running the company's UK operation. Before Hertz he was with the Orient Steam Navigation Company, joining the shipping line from school in North London as a cadet purser.

Quietly spoken, always courteous, however intense the pressure, Colin Marshall rapidly built up a reputation inside the airline for having an encyclopedic memory for faces and facts, and for being a stickler for detail. His managers would spend hours boning up on esoteric points before meetings with the CEO, only to be floored by something else. One reported at such a meeting that repeated shampooing of the carpets on board Concorde had caused them to shrink slightly. 'How much have they shrunk?' Marshall asked. 'By how many millimetres?' In his early days with the airline he worked his way methodically around the world network to meet and talk with staff in a demanding schedule for which his time with Orient Line, with which he sailed twenty-one times to Australia, had well prepared him.

Lord King and Gordon Dunlop were in complete contrast to Colin Marshall as personalities. Dunlop, a Scot trained as an accountant in Glasgow, was blunt and acerbic, with a gimlet eye for a column of figures. He had been on the manufacturing side of aviation with de Havilland and then Hawker Siddeley, had been chief executive of Commercial Union between 1972 and 1977, and had then worked with the Inchcape shipping group. When he parted company with BA at the end of 1988, to be succeeded as chief financial officer by Derek Stevens, he received £511 000 compensation, and a total of £895 000 including pension rights. Shareholders at the 1988–9 annual general meeting raised the question of the extent of the 'golden handshake', to be told by Lord King that Dunlop had a contract with three years' notice. The payment he received was in respect of loss of employment and pension rights, and was made only after taking legal advice. 'Our lawyers told us that if he were to take us to court, that was what he would get.'

Lord King had had a long career in industry before joining BA, most recently as chairman of the engineering group Babcock International, a position he had held since 1972. Born in Yorkshire in 1919 of humble beginnings, he started work on the shop floor and in his twenties formed his own company specialising in ball- and roller-bearings. Today he lives on 2000 acres in Leicestershire, has strong connections with the Belvoir hunt, drives a Bentley and, for its turning circle in the crowded metropolis, a London taxicab. When he first arrived at BA the chairman's executive Beechcraft was given the registration G-LKOW, but this was later changed since advertising the fact that Lord King of Wartnaby was flying was asking for trouble in a security-conscious world.

At the frequent press conferences at which British Airways set out its public stall during the first few years of Lord King's chairmanship, a period when the airline was seldom out of the news, he specialised in the short, sharp answer, making it clear that he had no time for what he considered to be a foolish question. It was an attitude which did not endear him to many journalists. Out of the public eye there was another *persona*, one of affability and charm.

His early days at the head of British Airways were recalled by Lord King in a lecture at the Institute of Directors in London, in June 1987, when he told his audience that nationalisation – in general – had not worked in Britain, and that since the end of World War 2 losses in the public-sector industries which government had written off exceeded £45 000 million – or at 1987 prices some £200 billion. At BA he had found a board of fifteen, selected by the Secretary of State and appointed by him for terms of three years only in the first instance.

I have no doubt that the appointees had exceptional skills in their chosen careers, but these were not necessarily relevant to the commercial success of British Airways.

I found also that the management had become accustomed to agreeing certain items with the sponsoring ministry *before* they had been put before the airline board. As someone used to a board being responsible to its shareholders, I found this situation needed – shall I say? – adjusting. Although unconnected with the issue of State ownership, another obstacle to generating efficiency and to happy relationships within the company was the residual problems still encountered from the merger of BOAC and BEA.

A second problem was the reluctance of the executive group of twelve of the senior managers to allow too much interference from an outside chairman. It was in fact like a large circle around which I went, trying to find a way in. In some ways, the feelings of those executives were perfectly understandable. After all, I was the fourth chairman of British Airways to be appointed by the government in eight years, and the eleventh in ten years of BOAC–BEA. On the staff side, it was well known that we were vastly overmanned. There was no possibility that, carrying such a weight of numbers, the airline could be properly competitive in the outside world. The organisation had become inward-looking, and the doctrine of Parkinson's Law was not unknown.

However, one of the company's greatest strengths was the pride that the vast majority of the employees had in the airline. What they lacked was the spirit of enterprise, and an understanding of the meaning of profit. When the time came to take practical steps to prepare the airline for the private sector, I was immensely encouraged by the way the employees as a whole responded to the measures that had to be taken. They knew in their hearts that it had to be done if the airline was to survive. At that time it was technically bankrupt, with debt in excess of £1 billion and a negative net worth.

It was a classic situation of a company which had become a self-serving organisation rather than reacting to the demands of the marketplace. Looking back, it is easy to see why British Airways at that time was the butt of so many sarcastic jokes. No wonder morale was low. It was imperative that we shook off the public-sector philosophy if we were to compete with the 160 or more airlines that were in our marketplace around the world – even though within this philosophy there were some admirable characteristics of public service which had passed down through the long history of the airline. Furthermore, it was obvious that without motivation we could not expect to raise the morale of our staff. That was essential if we were to improve our levels of customer service. For remember – in a service business quality is literally in the hands of every employee; there are no production lines, and no computer controls.

In order to ensure a maximum effort to change the image of the airline, we introduced a new livery and appearance, and new and different advertising. Perhaps the most important of all, we encouraged a much more open style of management – let's call it visible managment – providing leadership from the front. We had been known by the staff as 'balcony bosses'; the managers used to appear on balconies and look down on the staff, before hurrying back into their offices.

What general lessons did the British Airways experience teach for the future, Lord King asked. Firstly, that the government should not own and run any business – 'through no fault of Parliament, ministers, or civil servants, a government is not capable of running them effectively, efficiently, and profitably'. Secondly, the government should not both own and regulate an industry. And thirdly, the dominance of the Treasury made it very difficult for any government in power today to fund properly all the industries which it owned – the demands of other sections of the economy, and of the welfare state, were too great. 'It cannot be right, for instance, that British Airways, whilst it was government-owned, should have been delayed in getting permission to buy aircraft which it could prove it needed to further its business. The Transport Ministry may agree, but the Treasury may not, and therein lies the rub.'

Lord King expanded on these views in an interview with the author in late 1989, recounting how he had come to be appointed to the post of chairman. The first approaches came from John Nott and Norman Tebbit, two ministers in Mrs Thatcher's administration. Had it been at the personal invitation of the Prime Minister? 'I knew her, and had worked for her in the political arena, and so that suggestion is not too far from the truth.' After he had been at BA for a while, Lord King went to see the PM at 10 Downing Street, to tell her what, in his view, needed to be done to pull the ailing airline round. One of his major requirements was the freedom to pay his chief officers the going rate for outside industry, rather than the low levels set by the Boyle committee for board members of state-owned industries (the new chairman had discovered that his chief pilot was in fact being paid more than members of the airline's board). When Colin Marshall arrived as chief executive and Gordon Dunlop as chief financial officer, they were not given seats on the board immediately so that their salaries were not affected by the constraints of Boyle. It was a ploy which produced considerable heartburning among the Whitehall mandarins, but it provided an important pointer to the way in which BA was to be run in the future. Lord King told me:

> I started to look for a chief executive from the word go. It took eighteen months to two years to get Colin Marshall. I was looking for someone who was not only a good manager, but who also understood what the product was that we were selling – service, and that is what we found in him. I did not want an airline man; I wanted somebody who was able to look in at the business from outside.
>
> When I arrived at BA, I found that the airline was very good in so many ways, but it was overlooking the fact that the reason for its existence in a competitive

world was to serve customers, and to serve them better than anybody else was serving them. The company was immersed in a town hall syndrome, and that is the nature of a state-owned industry. The government had a lot to answer for in the way that they put the boards together for state-owned industries – quite often it is a parking lot for people like trade union leaders, economists, and it looks all right.

I do not know how successful I would have been sorting out the airline pre-Thatcher. I probably would have done something, but in fairness to my predecessors they were in a different world. I was fortunate in the government saying, 'Let us sort this thing out', and giving us the necessary backing. We introduced a little bit of Mr Micawber, some pride, and lo and behold, the people who were in the middle of the airline were thrilled with the opportunity of being given a lead.

One of the problems I recognised I had was that people were thinking, 'Well, he has been here nine months, and if we can hang on for another nine months he will have been here half of his three years, and he will then be getting ready to go.' This was the problem of the government-appointing chairmen and directors for three-year terms. I went back to government and said, 'This is no good. You had better appoint me for six years.' When that became known people said, 'Maybe we will have to listen to him after all.' I had to attract their attention, and I was fortunate in that I asked the advertising agents to come and see me, and they failed to do so. I eventually got a little cross about it. Then they turned up, and they were very nice people and their work was very good. But they said, 'We don't know why we are seeing the chairman. We do not normally deal with him.' I said I had asked them to see me not to look at their advertising, but to have a look at them and see what I thought about them. They lost out because it had occurred to me that they were deeply entrenched into the middle management of the airline. I followed that up by putting out the insurance to tender.

And so the staff right down the line began to take notice that we were going to get it right. All of the board members were busy men and competent people, but they were not in charge of it. One of my first encounters with the executive management was early on when the finance director put a lot of small-type stuff on the table and said, 'This has been approved by the Department of Trade, and if you will give it your blessing we will submit it to them.' I said I thought we would change that way of carrying on. It would be approved or disapproved by the BA board, and then sent to the Department of Trade for their approval.

The management tended to identify with the Department of Trade. One of the things which the Prime Minister had said to me was, 'There is no money, you know.' That had not been too difficult because the airline had always gone to the bank for more, and the overdraft was £1.2 billion at that time and could have gone on. I was able to find assets in and around the company – assets which were not really required in running the business, including one million square feet of offices in London, eighty aircraft, surplus this, that and the other. We actually raised out of the disposal of these assets £250 million, which provided the money to pay the redundancy to get rid of 23 000 people.

It was not a question of 23 000 people standing looking at another 23 000.

There were so many departments and divisions and operations which had been set up which were not required 365 days of the year. The people in the airline knew what was wrong, and we came up with the most generous terms we could. We had a complete survey made of what everybody's job was, and who they reported to. I was criticised for the generous terms, but I could not find anyone who could tell me what was generous if a man did not have a job. In the event, there was very little trouble; the airline did not come out on strike. The staff were sensible, and it was quite nice for a lot of people who wanted to retire, anyway. I have also been criticised for being ruthless at that time, but you must be careful of that word, because it means without compassion. I believe that the amount of compassion that we had was quite considerable.

A number of managers went. They were trying to prove that the old system and the old way of going on were OK. As far as I was concerned, I had gone there to put it right. So we changed the cast. And when we got that crust off, a lot of talent came up to the surface, talent that had been too nervous to stand up and be seen. The senior managers who went were capable people, but they were all caught up in what I might call a village atmosphere. They all belonged to one another. They were all in the same officers' mess. In fairness to them, it is very difficult for people to turn on a colleague.

The first twelve to eighteen months of my time at the airline were a problem, but after that I felt that I was getting to grips with it, and the staff knew that I was here to stay. And by the time the business was transferred to BA plc on vesting day in April 1984, we were beginning to make some real progress.

Although Mrs Thatcher and Lord King saw eye to eye, there was one well-publicised public falling out, in summer 1989, when, with the government trying to keep the lid on pay increases at 10% or less, the 1988–9 annual report of BA revealed that the chairman had been voted a rise equivalent to 116.6%, to £385 791. A BA engineer/shareholder got up at the AGM to suggest that his colleagues might receive similar increases, particularly as there was what he described as a 'haemorrhage' of engineers leaving the airline.

'I bet you could get more,' Lord King retorted. 'It's a free world. If you do not want us to be paid at all, we will do some other job. I didn't give myself this pay rise,' he went on. 'It was given to me by the directors of your company who decided that, based on proper research, it was something that began to compete with the rate for the job internationally that I was doing.'

A large part of his salary was made up of a bonus related to the company's profits. 'The justification for whatever is being paid to the people who run this airline profitably and well is in the results that you have before you [pre-tax profit for 1988–9 was £268 million, up 17.5%].' And pointing to Sir Colin Marshall, his chief executive, who had just been appointed one of two deputy chairmen, he added, 'I would rather like to hang on to him. He could get more elsewhere. It is a free world. It is your company and you can have some other deal. If you do not want us to be paid, we will do some other job.'

CHAPTER THREE

HOW THE HIGHLANDS WERE SAVED

The 10.15 am service from Glasgow has just landed on Benbecula after a 55-minute flight out over the mountains of Argyll and the Sea of the Hebrides, with the islands of Rum, Eigg, Muck and Skye glittering in the distance in the bright morning sunshine. Within a few seconds of the twin Rolls-Royce Dart 536-2 turboprop engines which power the British Aerospace 748, affectionately known to one and all as the Budgie, whining to a halt, a Post Office van has pulled up at the left-hand front door, an ambulance is at the back door on the same side, and an open truck is round the other side unloading passenger baggage and freight.

Inside the tiny terminal building, some eighty people provide an animated scene. All forty-four seats on the 748 are booked for the return trip to the mainland; the rest have either come to see them off, to do their shopping, to have their hair cut (there is a barber's shop in the terminal), or just to see the plane go, for the arrival and departure of the daily flight is a big event in this corner of the Western Isles, and the surface journey to Glasgow, by road and sea ferry, can take as long as ten hours. Just thirty-five minutes after touching down, Captain Ian Stevens and Senior First Officer Mark Berghouse start up for the return. It has been a hectic period for the three British Airways staff who man the station, for their duties are totally interchangeable, covering, among other things, passenger check-in, baggage and cargo heaving, manifesting and other documentation, driving the vehicles to and from the aircraft, seeing it off, and sending the signal to say that it has gone. During the turnround, the one member of cabin staff which the Budgie carries on this route has cleaned and tidied up the cabin ready for the arrival of the new load of passengers.

The Budgies which buzz busily between Glasgow, Benbecula, Aberdeen, Stornoway, Inverness, Wick, Kirkwall and Sumburgh provide a vital lifeline for remote communities in highlands and islands. Up to 10% of passengers on some flights, it is reckoned, are either going for, or returning from, hospital treatment in the big hospitals on the mainland, while the Budgies, with their ability to carry a tonne of freight in addition to their full passenger load, bring in essentials such as mail, newspapers, drugs, fresh fruit, car spares, and take out local produce which includes fresh fish, lobsters and woollens. It is a remarkable year-round operation which is only stopped by the *haar*, a sea fog peculiar to the Shetlands, and which continues throughout the tearing winds which sometimes hit the whole area and keep the sea ferries in their harbours. The pilots love the life – 'back to real flying' is the phrase which is frequently heard. They work hard, often being rostered for six services a day, but they like the opportunities for decision-making and the quality of the life off-duty.

Highlands Division of British Airways is a thriving airline within an airline, operating on first-name terms, profitable, and providing an essential and greatly appreciated service. Surveying it today, it is difficult to believe that in 1981 it almost died the death, a victim of the swingeing economies coming out of headquarters in London as the whole airline was painfully turned round to profit from its position of near-bankruptcy. How it was saved makes a fascinating story of human relationships, and is one that has been studied, and continues to be studied, by other airlines and by non-aviation companies all over the world.

Like the rest of BA, the Scottish operation was heavily overmanned and victim to outmoded and expensive working practices. It was flying elderly Viscount airliners, whose four turboprop engines were thirsty on fuel. There was a relaxed atmosphere, engendered by the feeling that losses would continue to be borne because of the large element of social-service flying which was undertaken to distant communities. Then, in 1981, the word came from Speedbird House, at Heathrow, that everything to the north of Glasgow was going to have to go, meaning a loss of 600 jobs and the handing over of the routes to other, smaller airlines. Management and trade unions rapidly came together and asked head office for time to work out their own survival plan. This was granted – three weeks. In fact it took six weeks to produce. To its credit, BA management down south, in the middle of a desperate hunt for every form of economy, agreed to give the plan a whirl, although there were very few in the airline who really believed that it would work. Its main planks were the breaking down of union demarcations on jobs so that employees became what was known as 'multi-functional', cutting staff numbers from 606 to 167, and getting rid of the Viscounts in favour of, initially, leased-in 748s. Highlands Division started life, phoenix-like, in April 1982.

The design for the revived division was drawn up between September and October 1981. Previously, the 'bottom line' had not been taken too seriously, but minds were cleared quickly when head office announced that routes which were unprofitable would have to go. A committee was established to draw up a survival plan, divided into a number of small, specialist working groups. Each of these looked at a different part of the division's operations, taking them apart in great detail to see how they worked, whether they could be improved, and whether they should be axed or not. Out of this came an agreement that there should be a much smaller unit, with aircraft which were efficient, and with 'multi-functional' crews – pilots and cabin staff who would do many other jobs as well, from checking in passengers to loading and unloading their baggage. Specialisation among the ground staff at BA's larger stations in Scotland was also abolished. Raw recruits were taken on for jobs such as check-in and cabin crew, with training completed in a couple of months. The result was a big increase in efficiency, enabling the division to keep the routes open, to develop traffic, and to begin to grow.

The management side of the committee which was established to work out the future was appointed by BA's head office in London, the trade union side by BATUC, the British Airways Trade Union Council. Initially the new set-up was experimental for a year, with the financial risks minimised through leasing, rather than buying, replacement aircraft for the thirsty four-engined Viscounts which had previously formed the backbone of the fleet. The participative group in Glasgow promised the management in London that they would turn the £6.1 million loss which had been recorded in the financial year 1980–1 around to profit in short order, and although they just missed it in the first year, they moved into the black marginally in the second year, and have stayed profitable ever since.

The fleet continued to expand, with a combination of leasing in and the more intensive use of existing aircraft – a task that was not the easiest in an area where some airports close from Saturday midday until the following Monday morning (Benbecula started to receive a Sunday service for the first time only in 1988). Diversification took place at weekends, therefore, with flights to Jersey, to Norway in summer, to Birmingham, and to Ireland. Freight charters were flown at night.

Staff at all levels were encouraged to put ideas for improving the division to the committee, and no such idea, however way out it might seem, was rejected until it had been looked at closely. The theory that management does not have any monopoly of good ideas was put to the test, and a number of improvements in the way that the division was run came by way of the rank-and-file workers. The ethos was 'working together' and, although management always retained the right to manage, it was careful not to overstep its autonomy. It remained aware that its bottom line was under constant scrutiny from London, and it accepted that it relied on BA as a whole to provide the benefits that stem from a large organisation.

In the selection of new aircraft, the management in Glasgow was able to make constructive suggestions to the aircraft-purchasing unit in London, the views of the pilots, and the staff who handle the planes on the ground being seriously considered.

The participative committee, established at the time of the rescue operation, still acts as the 'parliament' of Highlands Division, sitting once a month with its equal numbers of management and trade union representatives in sessions notable for their informal atmosphere. Decisions made there on the day-to-day running of the Division are implemented at once, without reference to anybody else in the airline. Then there is a business group, established to advise on items such as new routes, charter opportunities, replacement aircraft. Anybody working for the Division is able to come along with suggestions, or to hear how the business of the Division is doing. One of the Division's captains used his own computer to monitor the financial situation, while another spent some of his spare time organising efficient flying schedules. Crews and aircraft are treated as one operation, with all pilots and cabin crew rostered as equals.

Staff at the stations to which the Division flies were pared to the absolute minimum. Benbecula and Stornoway were reduced to three each, Wick two, the Shetlands six, Inverness seven. Alex Macrae, Station Manager at Stornoway, said, 'We are super multi-functional here. If it needs doing we do it – whatever the weather. We can have four seasons a day up here. If the aircraft doesn't get through, it can throw our schedules badly.' And Brian Kemp, Station Manager at Kirkwall, Orkney, commented, 'We have four full-time staff. We work most days, and only take days off when we can. We handle around twelve daily movements, including helicopters. Only fog stops operations, and that's rare. There are no strikes and little sickness – just a sense of community.'

Guided by advice from the Business Group which was established as part of the reorganisation, Highlands Division broke out of Scotland in a big way since the survival plan so that today over 50% of its total quarter of a million-plus annual passengers are carried on routes to the south and east. Its small and efficient 748 airliners have proved ideal on routes where jet equipment would offer too many seats and, therefore, return unacceptably high operating costs, and a number of airlines have beaten a path to the division's door to see if it could help them in their planning. Highlands Division aircraft are now seen in Manchester, Birmingham, Bergen, and also Berlin where two are based permanently, flying internal German routes for BA. The German service with 748s began in 1986 between Berlin, Bremen and Münster, and increased frequency over the following eighteen months saw traffic rise by a quarter, with Hanover added as a destination. Summer capacity between Manchester and Glasgow was increased 25%, with frequencies rising to five a day compared with the previous two per day by jet aircraft. Summer services on the 'Viking route' between Shetland and Bergen, Norway, proved so popular that the season was extended. The

Business Group looked round for ways of using the aircraft during the off-peak times at weekends and during the night. The latter problem was partly solved with a newspaper run from Glasgow to Ireland. For this the Glasgow engineering team strips out the seats on a 748 when it has finished its day's passenger runs so that the papers can be carried in the cabin. Then, in the early morning, the seats are fitted back again so that the Budgie can take on people once more.

With the fleet up to twelve 748s by summer 1988, and staff increasing to 225, Highlands Division was looking for a new and larger airliner type. The two main contenders were the French–Italian ATR-42 and the British Aerospace ATP (advanced turboprop), a larger descendant of the 748. While the 748 had carried the Division through the difficult period of the reorganisation as a jack-of-all-trades workhorse, it was becoming too small on some routes, while its technology was outdated by its newer rivals. Gerry Devine, manager of the Highlands Division, said:

> The crews do wonders for our image, but cabin noise-levels don't help, while galley equipment is far from ideal, and our ability to offer the high standards our customers expect is limited. Pilot conversion is doubly difficult, because the only 748 simulator is at Hyderabad, in Central India! Having said that, the Budgie has proved itself time and again in difficult conditions, and has led us into markets that have outgrown its capacity. We have been looking forward to the day when the Budgie can be replaced by something quieter, and which has the fuel efficiency to match the human efficiency which characterises the Highlands Division.

That 'something' was the 64-seat BAe Advanced Turbo-Prop, eight of which were ordered in a lease deal in the summer of 1988, with a further eight on option. Capital value of the order, options and spares was £120 million. The first of the ATPs went into service in November that year, and all eight were flying in BA colours by the summer of 1989 – the immediate availability of the type being one of the main reasons why the order went its way. Arrival of the first ATP signalled the start of a £1 million refurbishment programme for eight of the twelve 748s which were to remain with Highlands Division.

CHAPTER FOUR

INTO THE PRIVATE SECTOR

Moving British Airways from the public to the private sector was a long and highly-frustrating affair. The intention to denationalise BA was first announced by the Thatcher government in July 1979, and legislation to achieve it was passed in the Civil Aviation Act the following year. But it was February 1987 before the airline was at last successfully floated on the markets. In between, there were two major false starts and several minor ones. First of all, BA's floundering finances had to be moulded back into shape by its new management. The government had wanted to forge on with privatisation soon after the Civil Aviation Bill became law, but were baulked by the severe decline in BA's profits in the 1979–80 financial year, and by the large losses in the two fiscals which followed. No City of London institution, nor any member of the public, was going to invest money in an airline which was making such a rapid descent through extremely murky financial weather.

Looking back later at 1982, Gordon Dunlop, then the airline's Financial Director, said bluntly that at that time the company was technically bankrupt to the tune of £300 million, and that if it had been in the private sector, it would have gone through the bankruptcy courts. BA's management gritted its corporate teeth and applied itself to turning the airline round, a process which came off to the extent that by the summer of 1983 it was reporting profits of £77 million for the 1982–3 financial year. During 1983 also, BA repaid some £100 million of its borrowings without any assistance from the government. Lord King explained how it was done:

Simple, elementary stuff, you know. Home economics. Mr Micawber, you remember? Income a pound, expenditure 19s 6d, happiness, I think he said. And the other way – misery.

And that's the way it was then, but of course we were helped by the Margaret Thatcher government. She knew what she wanted, and gave one the freedom to get on and put it straight. So we set about reorganising the staff. That meant

23 000 people had to come out of the system, because there were 23 000 too many for what we were doing. Then there was no money, so we had to look around and see what assets there were in the company that were not really working and earning, and there were plenty of them. There were goodness knows how many hundreds of thousands of square feet of office space surplus to requirements, aircraft surplus, unprofitable routes. It was not really very different to mother's housekeeping money. There was so much for this, so much for that, so much for the other, and if there was anything left over, that might be holidays. What we did was to establish a situation where there was something over for holidays.

By the end of 1983 BA's downwards plunge had been halted, and the financial weather through which it had been battling was looking a lot clearer. So much so that the government put BA back into its queue of companies for privatising, registering it as a public limited company (plc) to give it the ability to trade as a Companies Act company, albeit still wholly owned by government. Nicholas Ridley, Secretary of State for Transport, rose in the House of Commons at that time to declaim, 'British Airways has remained too long preparing for take-off. It is a great tribute to Lord King, the BA board, and the entire staff of the airline that I can today position the airline on the runway for take-off into the private sector.'

But it is not uncommon in the airline industry for take-offs to be aborted, and the brakes went on this time because of the appearance on the runway of a blockage in the person of Sir Freddie Laker and a suit which he was bringing against British Airways and a number of other airlines and aerospace manufacturers, under the anti-trust laws in the United States. Had the case gone against BA and the others, multi-million dollar fines and costs could have been involved. With such uncertainty it would have been impossible to write the precisely-accurate prospectus demanded by British law of companies coming to the market. Privatisation went on to the back burner once again.

Freddie Laker said that he always wanted to go into aviation since the day as a schoolboy before the Second World War when he watched a German Zeppelin and an Imperial Airways HP 42 airliner flying over his native Kent. His post-war rise, to become the aviation entrepreneur best known and loved in Britain by the masses of ordinary people – 'the forgotten men' as he termed them – whom he flew on their annual package holidays to the sunshine resorts of the Mediterranean, has been well chronicled: how he bought a fleet of redundant Halifax bombers with a £30 000 loan from a friend he met in a public house, how he laid the foundations to a fortune by flying those aircraft through the Berlin airlift (choosing to carry coal, rather than flour, because he reasoned that coal, although dirty, would not clog up the instruments), how he threw up the managing directorship of British United Airways on the grounds that he spent more time negotiating with the trade unions over the strength of the tea in the canteen than he did running the airline, and how he started up his own airline, Laker Airways – or 'Fred Air' as he liked to call it – and then Skytrain.

Freddie Laker's commercial judgment was mostly as sharp as the proverbial tack. Living in a beautiful old brick and flint house near Guildford, with the extensive land which he then farmed stretching away outside the windows, he would sometimes drive his smartly restored 1928 Vauxhall 14 to the Duke of Wellington inn a mile or so along the road at East Horsley on Saturday lunchtimes. Parking the yellow and black car, with its discreet message for one of his tour companies lettered on the door – 'Live like a lord, on a Lord Brothers holiday' – in the pub carpark, he would open the lid of the box boot, which was full of package holiday brochures. While he was at the bar, subsequent arrivals would help themselves to the brochures, so that when he emerged the boot would be empty. Sir Freddie always reckoned to sell at least two holidays as a result of each lunchtime excursion for refreshment.

Skytrain, initially between Gatwick and New York, later to Los Angeles and Miami, was Sir Freddie's biggest idea for his forgotten man: cheap fares, no advance booking across the Atlantic, buy your meals on board, bring your own fish and chips if you wanted. It started as an amazing success in 1977, young backpackers queuing for seats for days under shelters made from sheets of plastic outside Laker Airways' London booking office at Victoria. Sir Freddie began a cheap-fare revolution among the airlines, which had its impact on the industry around the world. The big old-fashioned carriers soon became wise, matching the fare levels that Laker was offering. Sir Freddie's allegation was that some had concerted their actions to remove him from the scene, also that some had pressurised the US aircraft manufacturer McDonnell Douglas when that company, whose DC-10s Laker operated, prepared to help bail Sir Freddie out of the financial morass in which he later struggled. Sir Freddie went into liquidation in February 1982, and the legal processes began to grind soon after, with the lawyers talking about claims running into hundreds of millions of dollars against BA and other possible defendants. In the event, Sir Freddie settled out of court for $8 million, but not until almost two years after the optimistic government statement in the Commons that BA was positioned on the runway for take-off into the private sector.

By the time that the out-of-court deal was being finalised, BA's privatisation had been put off without any further target date in sight, for the airline's future had been muddied still further by a renegotiation of the Bermuda air services agreement which controls the pattern of operations over the North Atlantic between Britain and the United States. The original Bermuda agreement was signed by government negotiators from both countries in Bermuda as the Second World War came to an end. It stood as the blueprint until 1977, by which time both sides agreed that it was out-moded, and settled down to rewrite it so that it would take account of the tremendous expansion that there had been in air transport over the inter-vening thirty years. But rewriting it into what was known, at a long series of meetings in Washington and London, as Bermuda 2 was not a simple task. In the end it was signed in the middle of the night, right up against the deadline, with the UK threatening to close Heathrow to incoming US airliners if a conclusion was not reached. Both sides' airlines received new gateway points into each other's country; but six years later Bermuda 2 was deemed to need refining further. The talks between the UK and US government negotiating teams over what became known as 'Bermuda 2½'. were no less difficult than they had been for Bermuda 2. Once again they dragged on for months; once again BA was unable to write an accurate pros-pectus for flotation, as it was conceivable that it could have lost some of its lucrative North American gateways in the package that was being thrashed out. In the event, this did not happen, but it was only when Bermuda 2½ was out of the way that a firm bead could be taken once again on the bullseye of privatisation.

The delay had one big benefit for BA. It enabled the airline to build up its profitability still further from the turnround that had been noted by Nicholas Ridley in late 1983. In the financial year ended March 1984 pre-tax profit was £185 million; in the year ended March 1985 £168 million; and 1986 £183 million. By that year Lord King was in a position to state that in the previous four years his airline had produced operating surpluses of £943 million, and pre-tax profits of £609 million. During that time capital borrowings had fallen from £1053 million to £379 million, while capital and reserves had grown from a deficit of £195 million to a surplus of £480 million. The corporate aircraft was back on the runway again, and this time the light from the control tower was green.

But the delay had had a debilitating effect on the morale of the staff. Some became so disenchanted with the apparently endless hold-ups that they proposed a workers' buy-out. There were at least two such schemes, looking to the successful buy-out which had taken place shortly before at Vickers shipyard at Barrow. But Vickers was a much smaller company than BA, and it was extremely unlikely that government would have allowed such a scheme to be applied to a high-profile national flag-carrier such as BA.

As 1985 went on, the British Airways prospectus began to take shape, as did the plan of campaign to 'sell' the airline to potential investors. The government edict was that up to 10% of the share capital should be set aside for concessionary applications by employees (if such applications exceeded 10% they would still be met in full; if they did not reach 10% the balance up to that limit would be used to satisfy employee and pensioner priority applications at the full price); up to 20% of the share capital should be allocated to specifically-targeted overseas markets (there were public offerings in the United States and Canada, and private placements in Japan and Switzerland, but if there was heavy oversubscription in the UK public offer, the overseas amounts would be subject to clawback); and the balance was to be offered for sale in Britain, about 60% with institutions.

The run-up towards what was known as 'impact day' accelerated, with BA's management finding increasingly that they were required to have one foot on the accelerator and one foot on the brake. While they were deeply anxious to publicise the fitness of the airline for the forthcoming flotation, they were instructed by lawyers acting for the company and for the government that nothing must be said publicly to influence public opinion as to the future. A classic instance came when BA's 'super carrier' advertising campaign had a stewardess flying from the bottom left-hand corner of an advertisement to the top right-hand corner. The lawyers stopped it on grounds that an upwards-flying figure implied a rising level of profit. The advertisement was redrawn so that the stewardess flew level across the page. Just before Christmas 1986, BA did a promotion around the terminals at Heathrow when they gave away chocolate bars in the shape of Concorde to children; there was genuine fear in the publicity department that the lawyers might put a stop to that. After it was all over, David Burnside, BA Director of Public Affairs, reflected that BA got away with probably as much as it could get away with for a corporate advertising campaign. But in the future other companies would be even more restricted, he considered.

Airline management time was at a premium as the prospectus was put together on top of the routine tasks of keeping the airline running. The volume of legal work needing to be done was so vast that orthodox methods of communication by letter, Telex, telephone, were largely superseded by meetings, some of which went into almost constant session. They involved lawyers from BA, from the government, from the US, from Canada, merchant bankers from all over. What would normally have been a year's work was compressed into four and a half months between September 1986, when the government gave the signal for privatisation to start again, and 8 January 1987, when the Pathfinder Prospectus was issued. BA met government representatives every Thursday morning during that period to review the work of the week, and to decide on the course of action for the ensuing week – what meetings would be necessary. Those meetings were then set up by the merchant banks.

Quite often they were convened at 10 am and went through to the early hours of the following morning. The printers would then work through the night on a proof of what had been drawn up. Enormous care was taken not only to make sure that every word and every number that was going into the prospectus was true in itself, but was justified in being there. Searching examinations were made of the company's business, its assets, liabilities, or potential liabilities, to make sure that the description of the business to potential investors was honest.

In BA's case, the whole matter was made more complicated by the fact that the offer was to be made simultaneously in London, New York and Toronto in the form of a public offer, with private placings in Switzerland and Japan. At the same time, offers were made to the airline's employees in sixty-six countries, every one of which had a different legal system. In each case, BA had to investigate the local law and comply with it.

To continue the runway analogy, the BA corporate aircraft was now running along it at full speed and about to lift its nose into the air. By this time, as a result of the policies which were being pushed through by the successive Thatcher administrations, the British public was pretty conversant with the principle of returning nationalised industries to the private sector. In Britain some twenty big businesses, employing nearly half a million people, either had been, or were about to be, returned to the private sector. Six million Britons owned shares, twice the total seven years earlier, and nearly one-third of those six million owned shares in the enterprise in which they worked. But despite this favourable climate, would they buy into British Airways? British Gas and British Telecom, the two major privatisations before BA, had gone well, but they were stable businesses, largely unaffected by outside forces and with steady revenue streams. A big airline such as British Airways was something completely different. It had the glamour of travel which attaches to aviation, but it was also perceived as a highly cyclical industry whose financial and economic performance could be battered at short notice by forces far beyond its control.

There was the safety factor, for instance. In August 1985, the year before the privatisation thrust began, a Boeing 737 of the BA subsidiary British Airtours suffered a catastrophic failure in one of its engines as it ran down the runway at Manchester airport before take-off on a holiday flight to Corfu; in the smoke and fumes of the ensuing fire fifty-four people died. There were international factors. In the summer of 1986 BA's North Atlantic traffic in common with that of all other airlines on these routes, dropped off alarmingly after the Americans had raided Libya in reprisal for terrorist bomb outrages: potential tourists from the US stayed at home for fear that the Libyans would retaliate and they would be caught up. Business was depressed still further when the Soviet nuclear plant at Chernobyl caught fire, sending a cloud of radioactive material floating westwards over some of the areas where the tourists would have normally stayed. Then there was the future factor. Would the international oil price stay down, or would there be a new crisis, as there was in the 1970s, to skittle all BA's optimistic financial prognostications? How would deregulation (the sweeping away of rules on routes and fares) of the airline industry in the United States impact on BA and the other foreign airlines flying there? Would Europe follow suit, through liberalisation, bringing fares – and airline profitability – tumbling?

Time, or rather a shortage of it, was on BA's side, for whereas the Gas and Telecom campaigns had been drawn out, the BA campaign was a concertinaed affair, squeezed into a few months with little chance for anybody to become bored by constant repetition. On the other hand, the free-spending Christmas 1986 period intervened, leaving little over, it was feared in the BA camp, for a flutter on the Stock Exchange. The winter weather also frowned upon the campaign. BA's managers, led by Lord King and Colin Marshall, stumped the country, and abroad, at a series of what were called roadshows, giving the facts on privatisation to local businessmen, bank managers, institutional investors. This was during one of the worst winters on record; flights were delayed, invitees struggled to the shows muffled up in overcoats, scarves, Wellington boots. But at least they came. The interest in the launch was maintained at a high level, with BA, despite the constraints applied by the lawyers, running a high-profile campaign which made heavy use of the airline's Concordes.

City editors were flown in one from Heathrow to Edinburgh, where the aircraft circled above that city's fund managers before booming its way back south down the North Sea while the opinion-formers enjoyed strawberries and champagne – and sang for their supper by listening to a briefing on privatisation from BA's management and financial advisers. Then a Concorde flew low down the Thames, with Captain Brian Walpole giving a commentary over a radio link from the flight-deck to the crowds below, who were attending a big extravaganza on the river including a massive fireworks display. A barge with a large globe on it was moored on the Thames (and was stopped in the nick of time from breaking free from its moorings and floating off down river). Searchlights played. Balloons rose up into the overcast over St James's Park and Buckingham Palace. It all cost a mint of money, up to £400 000 for the two big Press events on Pathfinder Day and Impact Day alone, and it drew some criticism for extravagance. But it guaranteed the exposure that BA desperately needed, on the early TV shows, on the mid-evening news, on the Nine O'Clock News, on News At Ten. David Burnside, after it was all over, was of the opinion that it provided razzamatazz, interest, glamour on behalf of a glamorous industry. You could talk to any PR advertising agency in the world, and they would say that was very, very cost-effective. The criticism was just the usual ill-informed criticism you got when you were successful.

The great conundrum was at what price to set the shares. If they were priced too high, too few would buy and the issue would be in danger of becoming a flop. Set too low, and there would be a stampede, with further allegations in Parliament of a giveaway, as had happened with some of the earlier privatisations. Although the price was the government's final decision to make, everybody involved had their input. Like a spider sitting in the centre of a web, BA's management people were aware of the fine tremors coming in from outside on the subject, and particularly from the City editors who, they considered, it was vital to have on their side, agreeing with the price, if the flotation was to 'go'. A shading of 5p too much or 5p too little could have made all the difference between success and failure, but the word came back from the City that 125p would be a good competitive figure which could be recommended in the feature and leader pages. And so the decision was made to offer 720.2 million 25p ordinary shares at 125p each. In the event, the offer was heavily oversubscribed. Many applicants received a fraction of what they asked for; some received none at all. When all the dust had cleared, there were well over one million shareholders in BA, but with heavy profit-taking this figure reduced to some 400 000 within a year. (By the end of the 1988–9 financial year the airline's shareholders numbered 338 000. The great majority of these were resident in Britain, although over 10% of the shares were owned in North America, mostly in the United States in the form of American depository receipts. The shares were quoted on the London, New York and Toronto stock exchanges. The BA share register consisted largely of small investors, with the latest analysis of the company's share register at that time showing that nearly 98% of investors owned a thousand shares or less. Over three-quarters of BA's 48 760 employees at May 1989 were also shareholders in their airline, and many of the workforce were also members of the company's share option schemes, which provided opportunities for employee savings to be converted into ordinary shares in the future at a predetermined price.)

So British Airways was, at last, in the private sector, and the question now was, what would that achieve? Within a short space of time there had been an extraordinary sea change. Only a few years earlier the airline had been hemmed in by labour disputes, it was inefficient compared with many of its competitors, it was producing a poor product, and it had a humdrum image in the market place. Most of those disabilities had been cured during the run-up to privatisation, and now it ceased to have the high level of government support that it had enjoyed in the past. It was imperative that it should be able to react to problems in a much more speedy fashion than in the past.

This ability to react quickly to trends in a fast-moving industry was among the main attractions which BA's directors saw in the airline's new-found freedom from government control. Buying new aircraft and other major items of equipment involving the spending of large capital sums no longer had to be referred to the sponsoring department in Whitehall, and even to Cabinet. BA could now act in an entirely commercial manner, and the prospect was not a happy one for the airline's competitors, and particularly those registered in the UK. Many of them expressed fears of being swamped by the new BA, having had a whiff of what might be in store during the previous three years when the airline, despite still being tied to the government's apron strings, had begun to act very aggressively in the marketplace.

Lord King, as ever, did not mince words. He considered that the State, as the owner of businesses, was not a very good proprietor, with too many other calls on its time and its money. British Airways had been hamstrung in the past because Governments were poor owners. Now the airline, newly privatised, was free to go to the capital markets of the world to raise the money which it required, and this was independent of the government's budget for hospitals, roads, and other items of capital expenditure. 'We are free,' the chairman said. 'We can now get on and do it.'

There were, of course, some who were not as enthused. Clive Jenkins, General Secretary of the Association of Scientific, Technical and Managerial Staffs, considered that privatisation implied that the taxpayer, who had paid for the assets, was having large sums of money handed over to financiers – a policy which was against national interests. Jenkins was closely involved in a proposition for a workers' buy-out of the airline, and discussions did take place with a number of financial institutions to this end. Those institutions offered the cash needed, but against government opposition the idea withered and died. Jenkins' view was that a staff buy-out would have produced keener worker involvement in the running of the airline, and even after privatisation government capacity to control British Airways would remain absolute, because international air routes were settled by treaties between governments – so that the capacity of BA to be financially self-sufficient remained in the hands of the Secretary of State for Transport, reporting to Cabinet.

A new and aggressive BA emerged with the switch from the public to the private sector, and the flexing of corporate muscle was heard clearly in the summer of 1988 when Lord King addressed senior businessmen in central London. Pointing out that some £1.2 billion, or one-third, of the 1987–8 BA turnover had been earned on services in and out of continental Europe, the Chairman said,

> I should like to tell you that we are happy with the pace and pattern of that development. We are not. With a few honourable exceptions, of which the airlines of this country are the principal ones, the airlines of Western Europe are overgoverned, overprotected, and overregulated. As a result, the passenger is offered too few routes, flown by too few competitive airlines, and often at too high a price. The principal villain of the piece is state ownership. With relatively few exceptions, the airlines of Europe are wholly or predominantly owned by governments. As a result, it is difficult to get most European governments to accept that market forces should be allowed free play. And that airlines should

prosper or perish as they deserve. There is too much public money, too much political patronage; and too many personal careers are at stake.

So long as that is the case, I see no hope that the fresh air of free competition will be allowed to bring fares to the level that the costs of the most efficient carrier can bear. Because governments, like overprotecive parents, will always rush to shield their national airlines whenever they look like being bested by the boy next door. Why do so many European governments own and run airlines when customer and taxpayer alike would be much better off if they didn't? And why is civil aviation, almost alone amongst the transport industries of Europe, still treated like a highly dangerous animal that must be confined to a regulatory cage in case it escapes and bites somebody?

The theme that other European airlines should follow the BA example and privatise was developed in the summer of 1989 by Sir Colin Marshall (he was knighted in 1987) after BA asked eight European countries to approve cuts in fares and found support from only one of them – Spain. He said:

> This is another example of how the bulk of Europe's airline industry outside Britain is still a bastion of state bureaucracy and state ownership. The customer would benefit immensely from these price cuts. It is time for bureaucracy to give way to the market forces and allow airlines the freedom to set the competitive fares their customers are willing to pay, without government regulation.
>
> Even the draft proposals for the second phase of the European Economic Community liberalisation do not address this problem, and still permit EEC members to require sixty days' notice of proposals for fare changes. What price a really free and competitive aviation industry within Europe? If we want to reduce our fares tomorrow because of a trough in the market, we cannot. European governments do not allow airlines to price their services freely, and by the time that we have gone through the bureaucratic process the opportunity has gone, and the customer is the loser.

By the end of 1989 British Airways was, in fact, urging the European Commission to encourage all of its member states to move their airlines out of the public sector against the day, at the end of 1992, when trade frontiers between EC member states were due to be dismantled, and carriers would be able to compete freely with each other on fares and routes.

Airline competition, said Lord King, could not be truly open and fair while some airlines were supported or protected by their governments for outdated, nationalistic reasons, while others had to fend for themselves against competition from outside the Community.

> We compete daily with more than 100 foreign airlines and dozens of British carriers. Britain has the most active airline industry outside the United States. This is because the Government has decided it should not interfere with its day-to-day operation. The consumer should be the regulator. We thoroughly support this view. It is good for the customer and, as a company dedicated to providing our customers with what they want, we also benefit.

CHAPTER FIVE

TAKING OVER THE TARTAN AIRLINE

Sharing a fishing boat on a lake in North America during a break from a business trip in the summer of 1987, two senior airline managers, one from British Airways, the other from British Caledonian Airways, talked casually with each other about the spate of mergers and takeovers which was racking the industry. The conversation drifted from the general into the particular. His airline, the BCal man indicated, was in more serious economic trouble than was generally believed, and was open to offers from possible partners. It was a piece of news which aroused considerable interest in the BA man, and later that day he made a transatlantic call to Sir Colin Marshall in London. Sir Colin was also very interested, but before taking any precipitate action asked his manager to sleep on it and then obtain confirmation. The following morning the BA manager asked whether it was really true that BCal was seriously looking for a merger/takeover. Yes, said the BCal man, absolutely true, as his Chairman, Sir Adam Thomson, would confirm if an approach were made.

Back went this news to BA headquarters in London, and the first tentative contact was made at top level between the two airlines. Sir Adam, one of BCal's founders, said he would be pleased to talk to BA. An initial cash offer of £219 million was quickly agreed, and suddenly one morning in July pictures of Lord King and Sir Adam Thomson, beaming and shaking hands, were all over the front pages. The agreement was one of the best-kept secrets in the history of civil aviation in Britain. A select group of no more than a dozen people at the top in either airline were privy to the fact that negotiations were under way. Quite senior working directors were taken utterly by surprise when the announcement came, and not one newspaper, magazine, radio or television station got even a whiff that something big was in the air.

The fact that BCal was in trouble was well known throughout the industry. It was formed as Caledonian Airways by Sir Adam and a few friends back in the early 1960s as a 'respectable' charter airline, at a time when that sector of the industry had a racy reputation and numbered some cowboys among its leaders. It grew modestly with leased aircraft, serviced in the early days by Sabena, in Brussels, until it kicked off in 1970 when the committee that had been established under the late Sir Ronald Edwards by the government of the day to report on the future of the British air-transport industry recommended that there should be a 'second force' independent airline to compete with the then-nationalised BEA and BOAC. British United was then the largest independent, and the obvious choice for the second-force airline, but Thomson and his team mounted a takeover bid for BUA and, up against BOAC, won. The new airline was renamed British Caledonian by the end of 1970.

BCal inherited some scheduled routes from BUA. It also started some of its own, including Gatwick–New York and Gatwick–Los Angeles in 1973. Not everything went the new airline's way in those early days. Due to a severe thunderstorm over JFK, the inaugural flight to New York, carrying on board Lord Mountbatten, Lord Boyd-Carpenter, the then chairman of the CAA, and a number of other distinguished guests, had to divert into Boston on a Sunday afternoon. While haggis and tatties, Scottish pipers and a clan of Caledonian girls kicked their heels at Kennedy, there was no welcome at Logan, not even a set of steps for some little time to let the disgruntled passengers off the aircraft. BCal survived the inevitable ensuing publicity in good style, and the US routes were gradually building up when the first oil crisis of 1973–4 struck. BCal's management took the big decision to come off the new routes to cut growing losses, intending to go back on when economic times became rosier. But a Labour government then boxed the airline into South America and Africa, and it was not until 1 May 1985 that BCal went back on to the New York run. By that time it had expanded under Tory administrations into Dallas/Fort Worth, Houston and Atlanta, and into the fast-growing Pacific rim through a licence to Hong Kong.

But the shine that came with the early 1980s was dulled by the news on the aviation grapevine that the proposition to privatise British Airways was likely to become reality. The BCal board reasoned that a BA in the private sector would provide formidable opposition, and so it put forward to the CAA proposals which would give the independent airlines – and not just BCal – bigger networks, the routes to be transferred from BA. In BCal's case, there would have been some twenty routes in such a handover, and it would have meant the airline raising some £390 million in new finance for new airliners, additional staff and other commitments. The proposition was received favourably by BCal's backers in Scotland and in London, while the bank acting for the CAA confirmed that in their view it was a practical plan.

But then, according to Sir Adam Thomson, just as it looked as if the plan was to be accepted all round, the CAA suddenly scaled down the routes package. Although disappointed, the BCal management accepted it, but then the amended package was vetoed by Nicholas Ridley, then at the Department of Trade. Ridley, in turn, came up with a further proposition, which was for BCal to give up its routes to South America to BA, while BCal received Saudi Arabia from BA. Government also wanted BCal to give up its routes to Atlanta, Houston, and Dallas/Fort Worth.

Sir Adam felt at the time that the government had three alternatives: to implement the CAA's proposals; to allow BCal to transfer traffic from its base airport at Gatwick to the main London airport at Heathrow, to take advantage of through traffic there; and to merge BCal with BA. The government refused to accept any of these. The BCal chairman suspected that what the government was doing was to protect BA during the run-up towards privatisation, having agreed to write off its debts, and that the civil servants in the Department of Trade and the Department of Transport felt they had an obligation to look after 'their' airline. Guidance by the CAA, which had been established as an independent body to guide air transport, was being ignored.

In addition to the behind-the-scenes shenanigans alleged by Sir Adam, BCal, which was of too small a size to sit comfortably in an era of big airline battalions, but too large to be considered a 'niche carrier', that is to be able to concentrate on developing one small segment of the market, had been rattled by a series of economic blows which undermined its profitability. Only a series of sell-offs of its subsidiary companies, including an engine-repair factory in Scotland, travel companies, and a chain of hotels, helped to keep the corporate head above water. In 1983 BCal posted a profit of £2.5 million, but £1.9 million of this was from disposals; in 1984 the profit was £17.1 million, with £8.8 million coming from disposals; in 1985 £21.4 million, with £12.5 million from disposals; and in 1986 there was a loss of £19.3 million, but £25.4 million came from disposals.

The first of the economic blows fell in 1982 when Britain went to war with Argentina to regain possession of the Falkland Islands in the South Atlantic. The routes down to South America were among BCal's best but the war killed the traffic. The route to Libya was also a good one; this tailed off to a stop as British relations with that country gradually worsened, and with the US bombing in 1986. Then following the bombing, BCal suffered big traffic losses on its routes across the North Atlantic as American tourists, worried about reprisals, stayed at home. Sir Adam said at the time that a factor which accelerated this trend was a photograph which went round the world of a British bobby, previously looked upon by US visitors as benign, cheerful and always friendly, standing on guard at Heathrow nursing a submachine-gun.

Then the world oil industry went into a further decline, with a disastrous impact on BCal which had become known as the 'oilman's airline' as it had routes into three of the world's biggest oilfields – Texas, Scotland and Saudi Arabia, the last only recently gained in the routes' exchange ordered by the British government, which left BCal with Jeddah and Riyadh and BA with Rio de Janeiro and São Paulo. Not surprisingly BCal started to look round for partners who might help it spread costs. It lighted upon Sabena, the small and not particularly efficient state airline of Belgium which had itself just been involved in a lengthy, and abortive, series of talks towards a possible amalgamation with Scandinavian Airlines Systems (SAS), the consortium carrier of Sweden, Norway and Denmark – which was to enter the BA–BCal saga in a big way a little later. The talks between Sabena and SAS came to nothing, but BCal and Sabena did begin a joint service between Brussels, Gatwick and Atlanta. It was not a great success. The service used a Sabena Boeing 747 Combi, Sabena flight-deck crew, and cabin staff drawn jointly from the two airlines, but under Sabena direction, serving Sabena food and BCal wines. BCal had 62% of the seats blocked off to sell and market. The agreement between the two airlines was three inches thick and was thought to cover all eventualities, but in the event the problems of melding two cultures were underestimated, and there were tears in the galleys. The BCal trademark of the golden lion was seen by the Belgians as being similar to that on the crest used in the Flemish part of their country; rather than appearing to be favouring one section of the Belgian community against the other, this famous and traditional symbol of Scotland was discreetly dropped. BA quickly cancelled the agreement after the takeover.

Ironically, in view of later developments, when BA objected to the CAA about the joint service on the grounds that BCal was selling valuable passenger rights to Sabena, giving it a benefit to which it was not entitled, to the detriment of the UK, the CAA hearing was told by David Coltman, then managing director of BCal, that BA was using spoiling tactics 'fuelled by the arrogance of monopoly'. 'Monopoly' was what the critics of the BA–BCal takeover deal began to cry as soon as the news came out. BA had already identified the danger, and also the inevitability of being cast as the predatory big bad wolf which ate up innocent little Caledonian girls. Managers were warned against complacency, having it pointed out to them that the good reputation so laboriously built up over the previous five years could be gone in a matter of months if BA/BCal was seen by its passengers and the press to be degenerating into a large and uncaring airline.

Assuming that they could make it work, the takeover made a lot of sense to the management of BA. To their mind the monopoly accusation did not stand up. Seventy foreign airlines were flying into and out of Britain; the total passenger market in the UK during that year stood at 34.5 million, of which BA took 33% and BCal 5%. The main reason behind BA's takeover thinking was the trend which it had identified in the industry towards the mega-carrier, giants formed from amalgamations, particularly in the United States. In 1986 Texas Air Corp. (Continental, New York Air, People Express and Eastern Airlines) had carried 85.4 million passengers, the USAir group (US Air, Pacific Southwest and Piedmont) 55.6 million, Delta 53.2 million, American 51 million, United 50 million, Northwest 35.1 million, and TWA 24.1 million, whereas BA had carried 17 million, and with BCal would have carried a combined 19.3 million.

The BA management had identified eleven mergers between airlines in the United States during the first seven months of 1987. They argued that the world industry had yet to see anything like the full impact that these, and the others that went before them, were going to have on the world airline scene. Most of the US mega-carriers had not at that stage even fully realised themselves the extent of the market, and the massive financial clout that they could wield in it. When they did, they could be expected to turn it on in a big way, to the detriment of any airline not big and strong enough to stand up to them.

Benefits of the merger were listed as lower costs; the ability to build up higher load factors on BCal services – which, BA managers argued, were low because the airline lacked the sophistication of the computer-control systems which were available to BA; tighter monetary controls and improved yield per passenger kilometre for no fares increases; the more efficient use of crews and combined fleets of airliners; market opportunities from a wider network, with more connecting flights between the two airlines, instead of handing passengers on to competing airlines; and a greater ability to compete with those seventy foreign airlines which swarmed into and out of the Heathrow honeypot. BCal, the BA management said flatly, was also broke, and on top of that had orders in for £344 million worth of Airbus A320s and McDonnell Douglas MD-11s. It was patently going to have to merge with somebody soon, so why should not BA protect its rear and be that somebody?

Sir Colin Marshall quickly identified the problems of bringing the two airlines together. He assured the staff of BCal that what was going to happen was a merger, and that any aggravation which it caused would be shared by BA. The merged airline would in no way be a monopoly since the foreign airlines which flew into Britain had a majority of the traffic. The situation did not justify a reference to the Monopolies and Mergers Commission (MMC).

Under intense pressure in Parliament and from the independent airlines, Lord Young, Secretary of State for Trade and Industry, decided differently. After the Office of Fair Trading had rejected the proposition, Lord King and Sir Adam Thomson were invited to a 9 am meeting with the Minister, during which they were told that the original BA proposal to buy BCal as it stood was considered to be in some measure anti-competitive, and that the deal would therefore be referred to the MMC. Both airline chairmen expressed their fears to Lord Young that if the MMC took its usual length of time to consider this reference, BCal would be seriously damaged. With its future remaining in doubt, not only would passenger and freight bookings be affected, but the airline would be unable to approach with any certainty the period in the autumn when it traditionally signed complicated charter deals with a long list of travel companies for the package-holiday season beginning in the spring of 1988. Lord Young accepted these points, and ordered that the MMC should deal with the reference in three months, even going to the length of setting a deadline of 11 November for the report to be delivered.

Among those who watched the progress of the affair with close interest at that stage was Richard Branson, the British entrepreneur who had become a millionaire on the back of a pop music business, and who had then started his own airline, Virgin Atlantic, with ex-BA employees supplying much of the early expertise. In Branson's view, a merger would not make much difference. He believed that BA and BCal had never really competed, offering the same fares and the same quality of service on similar routes.

With the MMC in session and working hard against its early November deadline, it might have been thought that the dust would have had time to settle, but that was without taking into account two further extraordinary events which were to intervene – the appearance as a bidder for BCal of SAS, and the crash that October, on what was to become known as 'Black Monday', of world stock markets.

While the MMC took its evidence in London, 900 miles away in Stockholm Jan Carlzon, President of SAS, was putting together a startling offer. In his middle forties, Carlzon was well known in Scandinavian business circles as a radical thinker, with a flair for the flamboyant which kept him and his airline in the news. He first emerged to prominence with Vingressor, Sweden's largest inclusive-tour operator and a wholly-owned subsidiary of SAS, turning the company round from loss to profit in his first year as managing director. He then did a similar job on the Swedish domestic airline Linjeflyg, in which SAS has a 50% share, after which he became, at the age of forty, President and Chief Executive Officer of the whole SAS group. He joined SAS just as the airline had accumulated a two-year deficit of $30 million after reporting profits for each of the seventeen preceding years. Once again Carlzon effected a speedy financial turnround, investing £25 million in new products, services and training programmes, and preaching the gospel that individual staff members should take responsibility since the fleeting contact between employee and customer could make or break any company.

Carlzon launched a new livery for the SAS fleet, braving Nordic fury by doing away with the Viking ship head which had traditionally graced the side of the fuselage since the airline was formed in 1946. There were also new staff uniforms. When the new look was unveiled at Copenhagen airport, he appeared on the catwalk wearing the white tuxedo into which SAS pursers change when serving dinner on board. With management style like this, could not an injection of SAS cash into BCal revive the flagging UK airline? But there was more to the SAS interest than that. Carlzon had long believed that geographically his airline was out on a limb, serving just seventeen million people in the three countries which made up the partnership, and with the mainstream of European aviation business passing it by. A partnership with BCal, and a foot in the Gatwick base, would overcome this problem. The two networks could be amalgamated, giving SAS access to points in the world where it did not fly; the accent on business travel, stressed by both airlines, could be strengthened. No longer would SAS be in the danger, as he perceived it, of becoming a feeder airline to the larger carrier groupings which were likely to emerge in Europe as the tide of liberalisation spread.

SAS's flirtation with BCal was kept as good a secret as BA's original courtship, and it was not until seven days after the MMC had delivered itself of its verdict, in favour of the BA/BCal marriage, that SAS emerged into the open with the news that it was going to launch a partial offer. When the MMC decision was made public, it became obvious that BA's management had had to make considerable concessions before the Commission agreed that the merged airline would not be monopolistic. The 89-page report of its detailed inquiry, which had been led personally by the MMC Chairman, Sir Godfray Le Quesne, made it clear that BA's original bid would have been disallowed because it would have operated against the public interest. The MMC identified a number of possible detriments to the merger as originally proposed: removal of competition between BA and BCal would leave some routes on which there would be little competition for the merged airline; the airline would occupy a very powerful market position; it might present a threat to charter operators at Gatwick; and it might withhold from competing airlines the maintenance, repair and training facilities which had been provided to them by BCal. But the MMC also identified a number of benefits of a merger. It agreed that it would strengthen BA's ability to compete with big foreign airlines worldwide; it would bring financial savings through the merging of activities; it would remove any risk of the enforced liquidation of BCal or the breaking up of its business. The report commented:

> Liquidation or break-up would lead to the interruption of BCal's services, and possibly to the cessation of some of them. Several thousand BCal employees would face uncertainty, or even loss of employment. There must be some advantage in a solution which mitigates these possibilities. We have to assess the consequences to be expected of the merger proposals as they have now been

developed, balancing the advantages and the detriments which we have identified. Having done this, we conclude that the merger situation may be expected not to operate against the public interest.

The most important concession which BA had to make was to return to the CAA all BCal's licences to fly on UK domestic routes and prestigious and profitable routes to such European points as Paris, Brussels and Nice. BA also agreed to hand back route licences held by BCal but not being operated – Athens, Copenhagen, Hamburg, Oslo, Rome, Stockholm and Stuttgart. BA retained the right to apply for the reissue of those licences, although its applications would have no priority. It also agreed to withdraw appeals outstanding by BCal against the grant of route licences to its rival Air Europe for routes between Gatwick and Amsterdam, Brussels, Copenhagen, Frankfurt, Geneva, Munich, Paris and Zurich. (In the event, when the licences for the routes between Gatwick and Paris and Brussels came before the CAA in the summer of 1988, they licensed other airlines to take them over. BA then withdrew from the licence hearings for the remaining former BCal routes – to Nice, Oslo, Edinburgh and Manchester – Sir Colin Marshall commenting,

> We were left in no doubt that however sincere our motives and intentions, and no matter how vigorously we pursued our case, we had no prospects of securing any of the routes for which we were contending. We are not prepared to devote further costs and managerial time to what is becoming a pointless exercise.

In the judgement of the MMC, BA was also not allowed to oppose any application from another airline seeking to compete with it on any route where existing BA/BCal flights were not constrained by foreign governments under bilateral air agreements; the airline also had to agree to submit to a review by the CAA of all the routes flown by BCal to see whether further competition on them was desirable, and to surrender a minimum of 5000 take-off slots at Gatwick, spread 'reasonably' throughout the year. It would continue to offer to other airlines, without discrimination, maintenance and repair facilities made available to them at Gatwick by BCal; and it would merge the charter activities of British Airtours with BCal's charter activities, operating them under the Caledonian name. (BA later sold its half share in Cal Air, the BCal charter arm, for £10 million to the Rank Organisation, Cal Air's other shareholder.)

BCal's worth to BA had been considerably reduced by the undertakings it had been forced to give to the MMC. The question was, by how much? By how much had the original offer of £219 million been depreciated, also in the light of Black Monday, which had wiped billions off share values in general and caused BA's shares to drop 38% in particular? Just before the MMC reported, BCal sold its Copthorne hotel group to the Tara hotel group, an Aer Lingus subsidiary. There were rumours in the City of other,

Further development of Heathrow Airport, British Airways' main base, is crucial for the future, the airline considers.
Inset: British Airways has a marketing partnership with United Airlines, but its attempt during 1989 to buy into the major US airline came to nothing.

Above The run-up to privatisation of BA was a time of frantic publicity and razzmatazz to gain the ears, and pocketbooks, of investors. Lord King played his part as the bandwagon rolled.
Opposite top left As it was then; pilots Blake and Herne prepare to fly a scheduled service from London to Paris on 1 May, 1922, for one of BAs' predecessor airlines, Daimler Hire. Wrapped up against the cold in the open cockpit of the de Havilland 34 G-EBBS (one of them ensured warm feet by wearing spats), they are breaking all (present day) rules by smoking near the aircraft. *Top right* At Le Bourget, Paris, the crew take afternoon tea, still dressed

in their flying gear. Turn-rounds were swift (*see timetable above*), and G-EBBS set records during 1922 when it completed five single trips on the Croydon-Le Bourget route in one day. *Below* Back at base at Croydon airport, presumably at the end of a long flying day, pilots Blake and Herne enjoy a well-earned meal. The de Havilland 34, powered by one 450hp Napier Lion engine, had a cruising speed of 105mph. G-EBBS was destroyed in a crash in 1923.

LONDON - PARIS - LONDON (WEEK-DAYS & SUNDAYS)

ALL SERVICES OPERATED BY 3 - ENGINED AIRCRAFT, EQUIPPED WITH REFRESHMENT BUFFET

THE FLEET OF 4 - ENGINED AIRCRAFT AT PRESENT UNDER CONSTRUCTION WILL BE BROUGHT INTO SERVICE DURING THE WINTER PERIOD

FROM LONDON (Read down)						WEEK-DAYS						To LONDON (Read up)	
"A"	"B"											"C"	"D"
07.45	11.40	dep.	..	..	..	LONDON	AIRWAYS HOUSE	..	..	..	arr.	11.45	15.45
08.30	12.30	dep.	..	..	..	CROYDON	AERODROME	..	..	..	arr.	11.00	15.00
11.00	15.00	arr.	..	..	..	LE BOURGET	AERODROME	..	..	..	dep.	08.30	12.30
11.45	15.45	arr.	..	..	..	PARIS	AIRWAYS HOUSE	..	..	..	dep.	07.45	11.40

			SUNDAYS			To LONDON (Read up)
						"F"
ON	AIRWAYS HOUSE	..	..	..	arr.	15.45
N	AE					
RGET	AE					
	AI					

cluding Customs) formalities to be completed. Normally, loading of aircraft is completed 5 minutes before the time of

Opposite top As it is today; a BA Boeing 757 crew, Captain Clive Elton (right) and Senior First Officer Phil Bright, check in at the crew reporting centre at Heathrow before taking a scheduled service to Rome. Here, each discovers who is to be his partner on the flight deck, which aircraft they will be flying, and the stand where it is parked.

Opposite centre SFO Phil Bright accesses FICO, one of the many computers which back up BAs' flights today. FICO prints out information on winds and weather, diversionary airports along the route, navigation, and on any snags to the aircraft. *Below* On the flight deck of the 757 shortly before push-back from the terminal the crew carry out checks.

This page top FICO chatters out information by the yard. Up-to-date weather is also available from the display behind, while another computer, SWORD, calculates the fuel requirement.
Above SFO Phil Bright takes his turn to do the 'walk-round' and check the exterior.

The cutaway diagram of the flying boat carries the following labels:

Pitot tube for air speed indicator · Mast Head Light · Fixed aerial · 4 Pegasus air cooled engines, each of 740 rated horse-power · Mail Compartments · Variable pitch airscrews · Sleeping berths · Ship's Clerk · Dipole Aerial · Navigational Instruments, Blind flying equipment and Automatic Pilot · Radio Operator · First Officer · Captain · Mooring Hatch · CANOPUS · Retractable Bollard · Retractable Landing Light · Mooring Compartment · Metal Hull · Gangway to Control Room · Smoking cabin with accommodation for 7 passengers during the day and 4 at night · Passage way from main entrance · Men's Lavatory · Kitchen · Steward · Gangway to upper deck · Women's Lavatory · Adjustable chairs · Midship Cabin with accommodation for 3 passengers during the day and 4 at night

The most luxurious Fl

Length 88ft · Height from wate
Span 114ft · Weight fully loaded
The Empire Flying-Boat—

IMPERIAL

Top Interior 1936. Travel on the Empire
class flying boats had as much affinity
with the sea as with the air. Passengers
are seen here on the 'promenade deck'.

vi

Left Interior 1920s. The Handley Page
W.8 made its first flight in December,
1919. The seats were primitive, but the
fixtures luxurious – brocade curtains, a
mantelpiece clock, and candelabra.

Top Interior 1950s. The downstairs bar
of a Boeing Stratocruiser. *Above* Interior
1988. A BA 747-200, with seat-back
video.

Right Lord King (left), chairman of BA since 1981, seen here shaking hands with Sir Adam Thomson, chairman of BCal, when BAs' planned take over was announced.

Above Sir Freddie Laker shook up the traditional airlines in 1977, among them BA, with his revolutionary Skytrain low-fare transatlantic service. Here he poses before the first DC-10 flight, for which passengers queued to buy tickets shortly before take-off. *Left* Sir Colin Marshall, brought in by Lord King as chief executive in 1983, after a lengthy career in management with Hertz and Avis, strengthened BA as a market-oriented company, promoting 'Putting People First' campaigns among the staff, and seeing through a complete change in the airline's public 'image'.

foreign, suitors waiting in the wings if BA's new bid (it had twenty-one days from the MMC report to decide whether, and at what price, to renew) did not come up to BCal expectations. But Lord King and his board were not swayed by such considerations. They decided that an emasculated BCal was better than no BCal at all, and their valuation of it in that form was £119 million, a £100 million downgrading on the original bid.

When Jan Carlzon's SAS showed its hand, it was revealed as £130 million for the initial 23.5% voting stake in the BCal group, under an agreed recapitalisation package including the injection of £50 million new capital. BCal's board unanimously recommended it. Investors in Industry (3i), the investment group owned by UK clearing banks, would remain the largest single shareholder, with 23.53%. A BCal employee trust was to take a 7.19% stake in the airline. SAS said it would offer £20.44 per share in cash for 26.14% of BCal's existing shares, so that its £110 million total came close to BA's £119 million value in cash terms for the whole airline. At that time, the BA share offer was worth £148 million. However, in retrospect SAS was always on to a hiding to nothing in the battle of words, bids and counter-bids which followed. The first skirmish went to the Scandinavians, in that they had promised that there would be no redundancies if their bid for BCal was successful, whereas BA had let it slip that it would be looking for 2000 jobs, albeit from BA and BCal, if its bid went through.

The SAS campaign was led in London by Helge Lindberg, the airline's Norwegian Deputy President and former Chief Operating Officer, who was born in the British capital, and who was heard to say that he proposed to take up residence there until SAS had won a deal. But the writing was on the wall for SAS from the start on the issue of foreign control of a British airline, and the CAA remained clearly unimpressed by explanations as to what SAS proposed to do with BCal, given during a meeting which lasted two and a half hours on the day of the bid. Shortly afterwards, Paul Channon, Secretary of State for Transport, met Sir Adam Thomson and raised the possibility that he might use his powers under the Civil Aviation Act, 1982, to direct the revocation of licences in the event of a merger between BCal and SAS, and if control of BCal passed out of UK hands.

Sir Adam explained to the Minister the relationships between SAS and the governments of Sweden, Norway and Denmark, which sponsored the airline. SAS was owned three-sevenths by Sweden and two-sevenths by each of the other two countries. Each company in each country was 50% owned by its government and 50% by private interests. The airline received no subsidies, nor were purchasing decisions influenced by government interests. Channon, however, remained unimpressed, expressing the view that it would be neither right, nor conducive to fair competition between airlines in Britain, that, the government having earlier that same year finally achieved the privatisation of the British airline industry, a major

British airline should pass under control of an airline 'in which three other governments have a predominant interest'. Sir Adam asked the Minister to explain how BCal's case differed from those of Britannia and Monarch which, although foreign-controlled, had always been treated by the Department of Transport as British. There were, Channon argued, at least two important differences between the SAS–BCal proposal and the cases of Britannia and Monarch. First, neither was engaged predominantly in scheduled services, as was BCal; and secondly, neither was controlled by a foreign airline. Opportunities for British airlines to acquire a comparable involvement in any major Scandinavian airline would be 'restricted', he considered.

It soon became clear that a major factor behind the British government's unhappiness with the prospect of an SAS involvement in BCal was the fear that the United States would immediately argue that BCal could no longer be considered British, and that therefore the North Atlantic bilateral agreements, which had taken so long to thrash out, would have to be re-negotiated. Investors in Industry welcomed the SAS bid, and denied that it would involve a change to foreign control, while Helge Lindberg said, 'We want to keep BCal British, and British-controlled. We want to keep SAS Scandinavian, and Scandinavian-controlled.' He insisted that BCal would have only one Scandinavian director, in a non-executive capacity, on its board. And the joint shop stewards' committee at BCal attacked efforts by 'certain politicians and other vested interests' to stifle the SAS offer. They argued that BCal employees had struggled for seventeen years to give Britain an effective second-force airline, and had earned the right to their own choice. One straw in the wind in SAS's favour was Lord Young's view that the proposed link with BCal did not raise competition or public-interest issues.

Both sides lobbied Parliament, press and public opinion furiously as Britain ran up towards the Christmas/New Year close-down. David Burnside, BA's Director of Public Affairs, opined that it was the toughest PR battle BA ever had, and that privatisation was easy in comparison. Both BA and SAS indicated willingness to raise their offers, BA to £200 million, but matters were finally brought to a head immediately before the holiday with BCal calling for bids by midday. Lord King tabled a new bid of £250 million cash, and told 3i that it would be withdrawn if not accepted by 3 pm that same day; the offer had been raised because delay was seriously affecting BCal's trading position and the morale of its staff. Things then moved fast: BA's new bid was recommended by the BCal board, 3i sold its stake in BCal to BA, giving it a majority with the shares which BA already owned, and the deal was signed at 2.30 am in the London offices of BCal's financial advisers.

As he prepared to go back to report to Carlzon in Stockholm, Lindberg commented ruefully that SAS had been prepared to put in a new offer which would have been competitive with the £200 million offer from BA, but that they (BA) were prepared to pay anything, 'to firm up their monopoly'. In the end, BA seemed to have more to lose than SAS stood to gain. 'We knew from the outset that it would be a terrific uphill battle,' he added. 'We were in a takeover situation across national borders, in a heavily-regulated industry. We were the underdogs as partial bidders, restricted by air–political obstacles.' The question, he considered, had been decided where it rightly belonged – with the shareholders.

Lord King commented, 'We consider the price we have paid will be fully justified in the future trading and earning performance of BA. If we had failed to grasp this opportunity for expansion across the BCal route network, it might not arise again in the short- to medium-term future.'

As the ink dried on the deal, Sir Adam Thomson said, 'Clearly, I am disappointed that SAS did not win the day. That was what we were fighting for, but at the same time there was no way that BA, with £250 million on the table, could lose out.' The final bid from BA was 'very substantially higher' than the SAS proposal at that time and therefore the BCal board accepted it. Why did BA put the bid up so much more? 'Well, first and foremost, they didn't know what was in the other envelope.' (The other envelope in fact contained an SAS bid equivalent to £237 million.) What BA would gain from the takeover, in Sir Adam's view, were economies of skill in such areas as reservations systems and maintenance, and from the feed which the airline could develop overseas through having the two airlines together, rather than battling with each other.

SAS had initially proposed a take-up of 40% of the voting shares, but had had to come down to 23% at the end of the day. There was, he thought, no way that 23% of voting stock, and only one man on the board of BCal, could control the airline. But ministers did not necessarily believe that and he had felt 'aggression' coming from those he met during the takeover battle. The Secretary of State for Transport had been impatient in even listening to what BCal and SAS had to say, and had said he would reject their case after only ten minutes. There was, Sir Adam believed, some kind of national pride involved, and this ignored the fact that this was the way the air transport industry was going to go. There were going to be cross-border mergers and amalgamations over the next five or ten years. BCal–SAS just happened to be the first of these, but for some reason the British government did not like the project. SAS found themselves running into barriers with everything they tried to do, and BCal had a job getting a grudging acceptance out of the CAA.

It had been suggested in some quarters that the BA lobbying machine and Lord King's connections had had a lot to do with the political view of the proposed merger. Was there anything in that? Sir Adam said he considered there was a lot in the lobbying view. There was a lot of power in British Airways, which had been close to the government all way through, and also close to the civil servants, who recognised BA as 'their' airline, to be protected. And the same was the case with ministers.

In Sir Adam's view, the BCal staff had generally favoured the SAS/BCal deal. The airline had remained small enough to be a sort of family concern – something special to all its staff. But he had told the staff that the best thing to do was to get on with the new airline. And what would Sir Adam be doing? At that stage, he said, he had no idea, but he would not be sitting around doing nothing. He denied rumours that he was going to start another airline – it would be very difficult to do so in opposition to British Airways.

On the day that BA took control of British Caledonian, Sir Colin Marshall arrived at BCal's head offices, a glass-clad building with more affinity to Dallas, Texas, than Crawley, Sussex (and quickly placed on the market by BA), and spent four and a half hours with Sir Adam Thomson, his executive directors, and the chairmen and secretaries of the various staff panels. It gave him, he said afterwards, the opportunity of saying 'Hallo' and welcoming them to the British Airways organisation, and explaining to them how BA saw things happening. He received, he added, a very positive response. In addition to the welcome, Sir Colin gave the less palatable news of job losses – repeating the figure of 2000, of which some 500 would be outside the UK. But he pointed out that BA normally created around 3000 jobs a year in the UK, which should take care of the job-surplus issue.

He admitted that there were going to be a number of problem areas in trying to bring the two companies together, with matters of seniority to be resolved in particular, because of the different approaches that had been adopted by BA and BCal over the years. But the overriding factor was to ensure that both companies, in coming together, would maintain the high levels of customer service for which both had established good reputations.

The man who was given the daunting task of melding two airlines into one was Peter Owen, BA's Director of Operations. He recalled:

The brief was that we needed a cross-functional task-group to effect the merger. I went away and drew up some terms of reference. The essence was that speed was very important, bearing in mind the BEA/BOAC merger which had taken up to a decade to complete. It was clear that there was a high degree of potential for failure, seeing what had happened with airline mergers in North America. We also knew that some 70% of mergers – not just airlines – fail, with the major reason for failure being an inability to bridge the culture gap between companies. Quite clearly, there was a cultural difference between BA and BCal. BCal had always seen BA as a competitor. We had seen them as a competitor in licence applications, but not after that.

I set up fourteen task-forces to look at various business areas. Each had terms of reference and a leader, with an overall group co-ordinating their activities. I was very much concerned with the people issue, and established a 'culture club', which was mainly human resources. There was also a little group called the 'kitchen cabinet', consisting of my own team. We met every morning to discuss ideas and problems, and to talk about what was going on. BCal set up a similar structure, but until the whole deal received the nod there was a reticence on their part in giving us sensitive information. When the reference to the MMC came, there was a feeling outside the airline that we were not going to get away with it. BA did not accept this view, and we worked very hard on producing the report for the MMC in a short timescale. During the time that the MMC was considering the report, we continued to work to keep the momentum going, although we were operating in a vacuum at that time.

When the rival bid from SAS came in, we did not get any further help from BCal. After the MMC reported in favour of the merger, the mechanical side of it was bread and butter, but the people side was the key to it. Sorting out the management side was of vital importance. When we moved into BCal the problems that we had identified were worse than we had thought, but they were only problems of today and the potential of the company for tomorrow is tremendous. The main problem was a deteriorating financial situation, and the constraints on the operation of the airline that that presented – although not from a safety point of view. The different fleets of airliners had a ragbag of interior fittings and equipment, with very poor support systems. There was every evidence of a business that had been run down. Even the office furniture was mortgaged.

We had to set out to standardise the product. For instance, we found there was a 7% chance of BCal long-haul services not operating as scheduled. In BA this same chance is 1%. On the people side, they were facing a 40% cut in pay. Particularly hard hit were engineering, pilots and cabin crew. BCal had a method of working which was entirely different from BA's, particularly in the area of overtime. Our principle was to move everybody on to BA pay and conditions, and the way to do it was to be sensible and humane. We built in a cushioning mechanism over eighteen months to help this process. We were merging three airlines at Gatwick, with Airtours. The key to total integration was that Gatwick should be successful, with the new north terminal as the focus. Merging engineering was our biggest difficulty, because the working methods were so different. The staffs fitted in very well at Gatwick – in fact, a BA staff worry there was that they had been taken over by BCal. As far as BCal's managers were concerned, the difficulty was that they came from a small company where everybody knew what was going on, and where they had a broad range of responsibilities. Joining the much-larger BA presented them with certain problems and frustrations. Some ex-BCal managers felt they had joined a bureaucracy where they could not get things done as quickly as before.

On the day of the merger, we called for the senior BCal management, but not the board of directors, to assemble in the boardroom. There were a lot of ex-BA faces. There was a lot of shock around that morning, because they had been teetering on the brink of this for so long, up to four years, and the day had now arrived. The SAS thing had given them false hopes, so there was a lot of adrenalin flowing. But then I felt almost immediately that people wanted to get on and to know what the next stage was going to be. There was a bit of fear, and a bit of uncertainty, but also a lot of excitement about the future. It was a very civilised process compared with what it might have been.

The most common attitude among the BCal staff found by the team sent in by BA to begin the process of integration was one of apprehension, of being a David taken over by Goliath, of seeing their friendly, family, even cosy situation at Gatwick submerged within what were seen as the faceless battalions from Heathrow. Cabin staff were perhaps the saddest, sad about changing their tartan uniforms – which some American passengers had actually tried to buy off them on flights – for the blue, grey and red of BA, and sad to lose the Scottish image.

Remembering the lessons of the BEA/BOAC merger, which had been allowed to drag on for months, or in the case of a few departments even years, BA's management set out to achieve the joining together of the two airlines swiftly and cleanly, even if some toes and feelings became bruised in the process. The BCal identity was to be taken out without delay. There were even stories in the newspapers, indignantly denied by BA, that orders had gone out from BA's headquarters that the famous tartan material was to be summarily burned. In the event the tartan did survive, albeit in a small way. As part of its promises to the MMC, BA was to combine the activities of its charter subsidiary Airtours with BCal's charter activities, under the BCal name. Phoenix-like from the BCal ashes, Caledonian Airways therefore emerged, under Eamonn Mullaney who had been Managing Director of Airtours. Aircraft were given a new livery, a mixture of BA and BCal themes, but with a strong BCal flavour overall. While the fuselage was in BA's midnight blue and pearl grey, the red speedwing stripe was deleted to be replaced by a flash of BCal yellow. And on the tail fin the distinctive BCal lion stood rampant in the same colour. Cabin staff were allowed to wear the tartan, chosen from one of six Princess Mary weaves in the wardrobe.

There were to be few other concessions to the BCal past, however. As Airtours TriStars and Boeing 737s began to move through the paint shop to obtain their new Caledonian identity, the Airbus A320s which BCal had ordered were having their BCal colours replaced by BA livery by the manufacturers in Toulouse. At Gatwick teams of uniform fitters worked flat out weekdays and weekends to transfer 1000 BCal customer-contact and ground staff, 1300 BCal cabin crew and 700 BCal flight crew from BCal to BA outfits. The fitters, three from each airline, measured up fifty staff a day at the peak, to meet the deadline of having everybody in BA colours by the time the Queen opened the north terminal at Gatwick in March 1988, just under three months after the BA/BCal merger contract had been signed.

In the meantime, BA had embarked on the enormous and complex task of integrating the manpower of the two airlines. They faced a situation in which, particularly at stations abroad which were served by both airlines, there were now two people doing the same job. It was made clear that in such situations it would not necessarily be the BCal man or woman who went, and that below manager level staff reductions would be achieved by voluntary severance and early retirement. At BCal board level there was a clean sweep. Sir Adam Thomson, who was said to have received about £3 million for his shares and options in the sale of his airline, had not been expected to stay on, although had the SAS bid been successful he would have retained the chairmanship and his position as CEO for a further four years. But under pressure from BA, most of the best-known executive and non-executive directors also resigned from the beginning of February, although they were given two months to clear up their affairs. In their place BA appointed its own board to run the BCal group, led by Sir Colin Marshall.

Further down the line, every manager was being called in for interview, and in some cases – in both BA and BCal camps – careers that had extended over decades were cut short in the space of minutes. In the end about half of the 380 BCal managers were offered jobs by BA; most of the rest went on early retirement, many of them immediately, a few staying on for a while to help with the integration. Some seventy BA managers were offered 'voluntary severance'. This left the combined airline with 1700 managers, only 4% more than before BCal came on board. All of the UK permanent staff members of BCal were offered new jobs through contracts which spelled out pay and conditions agreed between the BA management and trade union representatives, although a rider was added that 'once staff are working to British Airways contracts, the process of handling any surplus due to rationalisation of the integrated workforce will begin'. BA went to considerable lengths to make uprooted BCal staff feel 'at home'. A theatre-style setting was hastily created in British Airtours' old hangar at Gatwick and there, in groups of 250 at a time, 6500 men and women sat through presentations on the theme 'Welcome to the New Future', a 90-minute talk and audio-visual show which gave them a flavour of BA and outlined plans for integrating the two companies.

Not everybody was happy with the plans. James Moorhouse, Conservative Euro MP, met representatives of BALPA and said that he was shocked by some of the things he had heard. The takeover was going to have more far-reaching consequences for BCal staff than anyone had forecast before the deal was struck.

> BCal captains, for one, will take some hard knocks. Some seventy-five of them will be required to train BA captains on to their own aircraft, only then to be made to serve under them. This will entail being demoted to first officer, and sitting in the right-hand seat. Quite apart from anything else, this doesn't look

like very good management practice, and can only make for bad blood on the flight-deck – hardly a recipe for high standards at this critical time.

BALPA had also told him about 'savage pay cuts' for BCal pilots of up to £10 000 a year.

> The unexpectedly strong line being taken by BA suggests that they have bitten off more than they can chew, having already paid out £250 million to ward off a BCal merger with SAS.

Almost immediately after the merger had been finalised, an objection surfaced from Peter Sutherland, the then Commissioner for Competition Policy at the Common Market's headquarters in Brussels. Urged on by some of the smaller independent UK airlines, who remained fearful of being squeezed out at Gatwick airport by a bigger, stronger BA, Sutherland focused on BA's route concentration into Europe and its share of take-off slots at Gatwick. BA took the EEC interest very seriously, for if it considered that the BA/BCal deal was anti-competitive, Brussels could conceivably invoke legislation to block it or, in Euro-ese, 'be free to re-evaluate the whole merger'. A series of informal discussions were held during the opening weeks of 1988 between managers from the airline and Peter Sutherland and his staff, culminating in a visit to Brussels by Sir Colin Marshall. The upshot was a number of commitments given to the European Commission by BA and accepted by the EEC. They included: BA would not appeal against any decision by the CAA if it turned down BA's applications to operate former BCal routes within the UK and to Paris, Brussels and Nice – routes that it had returned to the CAA under its undertakings to the MMC; BA would not, for the summer seasons 1989–92, use more than 25% of the slots at Gatwick airport; BA would not operate services under BCal licences between London and Athens, Copenhagen, Hamburg and Stuttgart. There were other points, ten in all, insisted upon by the European Commission, including an obligation upon BA to make a twice-yearly report to the Commission on the implementation of the commitments.

The intervention of the EEC in the affair was significant not only for BA but for all the other airlines of the EEC's member states, in that it was the first time that the Commission had flexed such a powerful muscle. It proved how serious Brussels was in its desire to see a completely liberalised European civil aviation scene by 1992; and it gave the smaller independent airlines heart as they joined the scramble for ex-BCal routes before the CAA in London during the summer of 1988. BA put a brave face on the outcome of its confrontation with Mr Sutherland, commenting that the commitments given 'are not expected to inhibit the implementation of the merger'. But the fact of the matter was that they had whittled down the worth of the merger to a degree, but BA was prepared to live with that and was pleased to have cleared what it hoped was the last of a lengthy series of merger hurdles.

Digesting the merger produced a hard time for British Airways from both the management and financial points of view. The joint airline's on-time performance out of the Gatwick base during the summer of 1988 was only poor, as managers, many of them specially drafted in from Heathrow, struggled to put the pieces of the jigsaw together. The financial reper-cussions produced echoes in the airline's 1988–9 annual report and accounts. The previous year's figures showed BCal to have lost £32 million in the first three months of 1988, limiting BA's profit to £228 million – although this was 41% higher than that achieved in 1986–7. They also showed the capital cost of the BCal acquisition to have totalled £353 mil-lion. This prompted one of BA's captains to query, in the airline's house newspaper, the whole value of the merger. The aircraft valuers Avmark had found the value of BCal's fleet to be less than book value, BCal routes had been lost, a promise to give up 5000 slots a year at Gatwick had been made, the BCal short-haul fleet was virtually all elderly BAC 1-11 aircraft, with limited airfield performance and noise problems in many European coun-tries. Flying staff from BCal had been retained at higher cost than those of British Airways, and with considerable problems of integration.

Gordon Dunlop, then BA's Chief Financial Officer, replied that the cost of acquiring BCal's shares was £253 million, including expenses. The bulk of this was paid in cash, much of it borrowed. Costs of severance, retrain-ing, contract cancellations, and bringing BCal's assets, including aircraft, to BA's standards, were estimated at £90 million. At the date of acqui-sition, BCal's liabilities less its tangible assets amounted to £10 million. This made up the total of £353 million.

People may ask what have we got for this price for a business which has no net tangible assets? The answer is simply a business (route network), people (an experienced workforce), and opportunities. We cannot put specific values on these, so we write the total off to reserves, but each undoubtedly has a value. The opportunities . . . include the potential to increase BCal's load factors and yields on their network to our own levels. There are prospective savings in operating and other overhead costs. BA's board remains confident that these benefits will be realised in terms of additional profits and will justify this outlay, having recognised that a number of BCal's routes in the UK and Europe will be lost.

The book value of the BCal fleet was below market. This has been taken care of in the £353 million. Having valued BCal's aircraft at market, it seemed only sensible to look at the market values of BA's fleet. This showed substantial undervaluation, and we took on to our balance sheet a conservative £277 mil-lion, which we credited to reserves. Our borrowing did increase in 1987–8 – partly on account of taking over BCal's borrowings, and for the cash borrowed to purchase BCal's shares. It is up to all of us to exploit the advantages and opportunities of the merger, and to realise the potential benefits that there are.

By the end of the 1988–9 financial year, on 31 March 1989, the process of absorbing the financial losses of BCal was complete, according to Lord King. He told shareholders:

BCal has now been fully integrated into British Airways, and we have already begun to benefit from the expansion. The merger has been no easy task. Unifying the two companies, with all the human and operational consequences, and consolidating the combined airline services in Gatwick's new North Terminal, required an outstanding effort by management and staff in many areas.

This was the close of the immediate BCal saga. For the longer term, the combined management of the newly-forged airline could get down to the lengthy and complex business of moulding the merged companies into shape to compete with the menacing US mega-carriers – which was how it had all begun during that chance conversation in a fishing boat almost twenty-four months before.

CHAPTER SIX

THE MARKETEERS:
CHANGING THE IMAGE

Strange and highly secret things went on in one of the hangars at British Airways' main engineering base at Heathrow airport during the winter of 1984–5. The windows had been painted over so that nobody passing could see in, and security men let by only the fifty BA staff who were engaged on the hush-hush project within. That project was the airline's new look – a change which every airline makes from time to time – which flowered publicly, appropriately enough, in the early spring of 1985. At £42 million it was the most adventurous effort to market BA in the history of the company, embodying as it did a total alteration of 'image' to go with the new style which Lord King, Colin Marshall and their managers had been working to introduce.

In the hangar one of the airline's Boeings was being repainted in dark blue, grey and red, the revised colours which were to run right through the airline, on everything from uniforms to ticket wallets, from cars and trucks to sales shops, from luggage labels to visiting cards. It was a clean sweep of the former combination of red, white and blue. Even the dark-blue speedbird motif, dating back to the old Imperial Airways of the 1930s, carried on by BOAC, and which had survived the merger with BEA, was despatched, to be replaced with the 'speedwing', a half arrowhead with a long body, all in red, which ran along the side of the aircraft fuselage, the tick of the arrow matching the angle of the bar in the quartered union flag on the tail. The speedwing appeared on all the many other items which were revamped. Inevitably there were criticisms of the new look: dropping the speedbird and old colour scheme which had majored on the national colours was bound to be controversial, but BA's management felt that the former style, which had been around since 1973, was too reminiscent of the era of Carnaby Street, long gone and outdated and certainly not in tune with the cool, caring, market-led organisation which, they hoped, was how BA was now perceived. They restored the word Airways after British on the side of the aircraft – the decision to drop it had itself been a matter for argument two years earlier – but they ran into trouble with a decision to use the airline's crest and motto 'To Fly, To Serve' on the aircraft tail fins. The Director of the Society of Industrial Artists and Designers thought the use of the crest was wholly inappropriate for an airline 'and more in keeping with a packet of cigarettes'.

The designer of the new BA corporate image was Landor Associates, an American company based in San Francisco, a fact which might just have accounted, some uncharitable commentators suggested at the time, for the dudgeon among designers based in Britain. From its headquarters on the old ferry-boat *Klamath*, moored in San Francisco harbour, Landor had revamped seventeen airline liveries before it clinched the BA contract, reputedly worth around £2 million. The work took the company, which is the largest design consultancy in the world, eighteen months of intensive effort, with a team of thirty of its senior people involved in a thousand meetings with all the various levels of BA's management. Landor took the BA statement, 'Our corporate goal is to become the best airline in the world', as its starting point, and in its suggested design changes tried to move the airline away from the competition, all of which, it was considered, were begining to have a similar look. The single word, 'British', on the side was thought to be too nationalistic, and possibly offensive in some third-world countries. Other aims were to signal a complete break from the past, and to extol the virtues of precision, professionalism, technological innovation and competence. These sweeping parameters established, Landor then got down to detailed design development.

As many as 300 design possibilities were drawn up. A great deal of effort was expended on finding a new symbol for the airline. Various versions of the Union Jack were considered, as was a globe drawn by computer graphics, as was the old speedbird, as were the letters BA and other combinations of words, among them 'British Air'. Finally, three choices were shortlisted, to be market-researched in ten countries, Britain, the United States, France, Germany, Japan, Australia, India, Kenya, Saudi Arabia and South Africa. Response to the designs was tested by Landor's research department against a number of parameters – British, reliable, high-tech, distinctive, modern, exciting, and warm – and the favourite scored on all of these, with the exception of 'warm', where the difference between it and the old design was considered to be too negligible to worry about. When the results were made public, reaction centred largely on the speedwing line, which Landor saw as something which reflected the hard-edged qualities of precision and which gave the impression of a laser, and on the disappearance of the speedbird. Landor's people considered the bird image was outmoded, and a passé piece of airline symbolism indicating what everybody knew in the 1980s, that man could fly. This did not, however, prevent a petition to save it being drawn up and presented by members of BA's staff.

The overall colour scheme was accepted publicly without too much fuss. Pearl grey had been used for the tops of aircraft as a way of distancing BA from the colour schemes of many other airlines which used white paint (Landor had proposed silver tops originally, but this was dropped when found to be impracticable from the technical point of view). 'British Airways' came back on to the sides of the aircraft in place of 'British' as this was thought to indicate a more saleable proposition with privatisation coming up.

Landor's philosophy in approaching the BA brief was that Saatchi and Saatchi's advertising campaign, 'The world's favourite airline', which had been running for a while, was so good that the interiors of the airline's aircraft were not up to the promise that it made. Landor's people talked to management and to the employees, particularly those in daily contact with the travelling public. They travelled all over the world, asking questions about how BA was perceived as an airline, finding out what was considered good, and what was bad. After three months of this process Landor reported back to BA with an analysis of its image.

Then the business of design began. Landor knew from its experience that staff reaction to changes of image was important, but felt that much of the inevitable scepticism about the changes had already been blunted by the fact that staff had been going through a series of educational courses called 'Putting People First'. Some 500 sketches of possible designs were produced, ranging from total changes of the existing livery to close adaptations of it. The scale of the task was enormous, for the new design had to be seen to link hundreds of aircraft, thousands of ground vehicles, and multifarious other items from carpets to curtains.

Undoubtedly the most daunting challenge was the aircraft fleet, mainly because each plane was a large canvas for the artist and was also the major item of which the public was conscious. The interior was designed to be relaxing and comfortable; the British Airways coat of arms, with its motto 'To Fly, To Serve', was put on the fin, largely because the commitment to serve the public was what the 'new' British Airways was all about; the speedwing was chosen because its thin red line gave an idea of precision, high-tech and quality in aircraft maintenance.

BA's fleet of seven supersonic Concorde airliners received special treatment, not only because they were patronised by the airline's top eche-lon of business passengers, but because there was a good technical reason why they could not be painted red, blue and grey, like all their subsonic brothers. BA's engineers pointed out that, because of the aircraft's high speed at high altitude, it had to be painted a colour which reflected the heat which it produced – and so Concordes came out white all over, except for the red speedwing down the sides, a flash of blue and red on the fin, and the silver coat of arms. At the end of it all, Landor reckoned it had given British Airways a new suit of clothes which would last a good ten years before looking the least bit outdated.

It was not until the summer of 1985 that the first Concorde in the new and specialised livery emerged from the BA engineering base, after a further close-to-the-chest refurbishing operation. This was G-BOAG, an addition to the fleet to bring the total of supersonic aircraft to seven. With the popularity of the London–New York and London–Washington/Miami routes, plus the fact that the capacity of one aircraft was being taken up by charters, ranging from trips round the world to trips round the Bay of Biscay, BA had found itself becoming short of Concorde capacity. Coincidentally with the decision to renew the livery, the decision to bring Alpha George back into service was made. Since 1982 this aircraft had languished in one of BA's hangars after being withdrawn from service because there was not at that time enough business to keep it flying. As a result, by 1985 it had performed only 1400 flight hours, while the other six each had around 8500 hours 'on the clock'. But bringing it back up to operational standard was a massive task, involving 23 000 man-hours, for G-BOAG had not only been 'cannibalised' for spares for her six sisters, but she had fallen badly behind in the modification programme. When she finally rolled out in mid-1985, led by the BA pipe band, she had not only been brought right up to engineering peak, but she was the vehicle for BA's livery change. Lord King said, 'It's like a lady with a new dress. It is time we had new colours, and we in the airline, and all our passengers, will feel better for it.'

The main interest was to see what the designers had done with the inside. The overall impression was grey – grey carpeting relieved with a thin red stripe running the length of the central aisle, grey leather on the bulkheads, grey leather and fabric covering the newly-designed seats. The seats were a different shape from the old, two inches lower and slightly rounded at the top of the back. The intention was to give an impression of more space in Concorde's long, tube-like interior, and this it succeeded in doing. It also brought some grumbles from Concorde passengers that it had destroyed their comparative privacy, so that passengers sitting behind could now see through into their seat row to glimpse the industrial secrets in the papers they were reading on the flight. A further criticism was that the grey colour scheme was too monochrome. John Diefenbach, the head of Landor Associates, replied that the intention was that the clothes of the passengers, and the new uniforms of the cabin staff, would provide the essential colour, and although that proved to be the case to a degree, BA quietly introduced an element of colour into the décor a couple of years later.

A further change to the revamped Concordes was the introduction on to the cabin bulkheads at the front and in the middle of each aircraft of digitalised information panels to replace the smaller earlier version which had simply given the speed over the ground in terms of Mach number. The replacement gave increased amounts of information, including height and outside temperature, and a 'thank you for flying Concorde' message on landing, but it was some time before the technical bugs were sorted out and a number of the earlier flights crossed the Atlantic with the screens blank.

New uniforms for pilots, cabin staff, engineers, motor-transport drivers – everybody whose jobs brought them into contact with the public – were among the final pieces of this gigantic marketing jigsaw puzzle to be slipped into place. But even after launch it took the best part of two years to bring it all into being. Technically, the task was a forbidding one. For instance, to cover the 400 seats in each of the airline's twenty-eight B747s took half a mile of the new cloth. Throughout the fleet, there were 33 000 aircraft seats to be renewed or refitted. New interior layouts, with better galleys, toilets and baggage-stowage areas, were built into the 'jumbo' fleet at Heathrow, and under subcontract in Hong Kong. Once the engineers moved into their stride, they were refurnishing airliners of B757 size at the rate of one every three days, but even so it was late in 1987 before the last examples of the old 'Carnaby Street' colours finally vanished from the flight line.

The marketeers in BA, with Jim Harris, Marketing Director, at their head, provided much of the impetus for all these alterations. From 1 February 1983, the day Colin Marshall arrived at the airline, BA underwent a dramatic and fundamental sea-change, becoming 'market-led' – that is, with the marketing department making the innovatory running – rather than planning and operations-led, as had traditionally been the case. One of the new Chief Executive's first acts on the day that he moved into his office at BA's headquarters was to call in Harris and instruct him to form a Marketing Policy Group, with the brief to spearhead the sweeping alterations in the airline's internal organisation, and its perception by the public, which he wanted to see made. Marketing quickly became responsible for customer service in all areas except cabin crew, although even there they began to have considerable input into the service standards that cabin crew offered to passengers, right down to the types of meals, wines and newspapers. The department also became responsible for the corporate image. The changes inevitably produced internal rumblings, but Marshall was quick to push through his plan to have the various major departments within the airline working together rather than, as was graphically described by one senior manager closely involved with the changes, 'acting like a series of individual smokestacks'.

By 1983, most of the cost-cutting necessary to turn BA round had been completed. But this period had inevitably placed severe restrictions on capital expenditure so that there was a lot of catching up to do in terms of both improving the existing services and developing new ones, while staff morale, at a low ebb, needed to be boosted. The corporate advertising account was switched from Foote, Cone and Belding, which had held it for many years, to Saatchi and Saatchi, which had successfully masterminded the Conservative election advertising. One of Saatchi's first acts for BA was to coin the new slogan. 'The world's favourite airline' was chosen by the BA management from a long list of alternatives on the grounds that it could be justified factually because BA was carrying more international passengers than any other airline. The management was not so sure about the use of the word 'favourite' in its slightly shaded form – that BA was the airline which people loved to fly – but they hoped that with the marketing initiatives that were planned, BA would grow into that. The slogan was, the management thought, 'aspirational'.

With a lot of work needed to improve the airline, an interest-holding exercise was needed. This manifested itself to the public with a striking television advertisement 'Manhattan Landing'. In this the island of Manhattan – skyscrapers, the Statue of Liberty, and all – was seen flying over London, to the amazement of people in the streets, to make a touchdown at Heathrow, the message intended being that BA was a big enough airline to be carrying the entire population of New York across the Atlantic each year. During the time bought by this campaign, BA spruced up its shuttle services on the main domestic UK routes, moved towards spreading Super Club on to all the long-haul routes instead of just the North Atlantic, and started work on the new corporate identity. The internal morale crisis was addressed through a series of seminars which everybody in the airline, from everywhere in the world, attended – notably 'Putting People First'. Bought in from Scandinavia, where something similar has been used by SAS to motivate its staff, and adapted for BA use, the programme, which had a distinct marketing emphasis, urged BA workers to be friendlier towards their customers. Each Putting People First seminar lasted over two days. On the first morning the resistance among some British members of staff who objected to being lectured in what they saw as an American whizz-kid manner was palpable, but this attitude generally broke down as the seminar progressed. Putting People First was judged a success by BA management not only because the programme gave staff a new direction and started to restore morale, but because it brought workers together from areas of the airline which would never normally meet.

The bar on recruitment which had been in force while BA was going through its slimming process was first waived for new cabin crew – and a new breed of cabin crew. The stiff educational requirements previously demanded were dropped; personality became important. 'Sparkly' was the new watchword, and young men and women who sparkled during the interview generally got the job. Old attitudes were changing as BA moved rapidly, and sometimes painfully, towards being a born-again airline. But even when the rings on the sleeve denoting rank were dropped with the change of uniform for everybody but flight crews there was scarcely a murmur, although management had identified this hangover from World War 2 days as being a potential minefield of protest.

Marketing, along with Saatchi and Saatchi, began battering away at the public perception of BA in a series of TV commercials which were so outstanding in their originality that viewers either loved or hated them. But what the majority of the public did not do was forget them, nor the airline from which they originated. The target was therefore struck, for the BA marketeers wanted something that broke away from the bland advertising of most of their competitors, which they saw as 'all the same – in-cabin, upbeat music, lots of girls'. The avuncular and very typically British voice of the actor Robert Morley was utilised for the first of the series, which jokily showed well-known people, including Omar Sharif, Joan Collins, and US football stars, expressing rage and disappointment when discovering they had been booked on an airline other than BA. Morley had been used by BA in the United States as far back as 1971, both in a series of TV ads and as a recorded telephone voice asking callers to hang on, 'because those chaps at British Airways are busy at the moment'. Many of the British community in the US hated the use of Morley as giving a tourist-eye impression of their country, but Americans loved him, and a lot of them believed he was actually chairman of the airline.

'Oh the Disappointment', as the Omar Sharif *et al.* ad was called, was followed by others just as mould-breaking, all designed to portray BA as a warm and caring, technically advanced and worldwide carrier. A commercial for Super Club showed the roof of an airliner being opened to allow one small bird to fly away. Astronauts were portrayed marooned on some distant planet, peopled by fantastic creatures breathing fire. The travellers go into the BA office on the planet to book their passage back to earth. 'Smoking or non-smoking?' the ticket clerk enquires. 'Non-smoking,' reply the astronauts, viewing their fellow passengers with trepidation. Stewards and stewardesses who could fly like Superman were introduced to further the caring theme. A BA girl enjoying a cup of coffee on the Eiffel Tower in Paris sees a passenger's bag fall over the side, flies down, and retrieves the contents after it has gone through the boot of a car. A BA steward sees a truck-load of footballs spilled over a motorway, holding up two business passengers on their way to catch their flight. Using Superman powers, he boots them all back into the truck. Then came the 'Let me through, I'm a British Airways steward/stewardess' series, in which a passenger with red wine spilled down his shirt was provided with a replacement by a BA man passing by. The ads made the desired impact. One viewer wrote to the airline, 'If that silly girl hadn't stopped to finish her cup of coffee, she would have caught the man's bag before it hit the car', while 'Let me through . . .' became something of a national catchphrase.

The marketeers played a big part in the privatisation campaign, and the TV commercial in which famous buildings, including London's Albert Hall and the Sydney Opera House, doffed their roofs to BA was a further marketing/Saatchi extravaganza. What the department had learned from the turnround of the business was the need to be immediately aware of, and to react quickly to, events and public opinion. This lesson was applied to the chronic downturn of business which followed the Libyan bombing and Chernobyl nuclear disaster in April 1986. By the following month, one million Americans had entered BA's free 'Go For It, America' lottery, and by June 12 000 of them were on free trips to London. A few of them took tea with the Prime Minister, at No. 10 Downing Street. One won the use of Concorde for himself and ninety-nine friends for a day.

What BA's marketing department did after the arrival of Colin Marshall was to do away with the traditional mystique surrounding airlines and to apply the ethos of the fast-moving consumer-goods industry to the business. Up to a dozen managers skilled in such selling were recruited from companies such as Unilever and Campbell's Soups, under a Head of Products and Brands, Mike Batt, himself from the confectionery firm Mars. Branding the product began early in 1988 with the launch of Club World and Club Europe in a film studio in a run-down area of London just south of the Thames, to the accompaniment of laser lights, audio-visuals, and pop music of an intensity on the threshold of pain.

A year after the launch of the new club classes, BA's marketeers sprang a revitalised first-class product on its customers, the venue this time being rather more up-market – a conference centre just across the road from Westminster Abbey. The airline had put two years' work into the relaunch, the target of which was a greater share than the £225 million already earned each year from the total market for first-class travel on the long-haul routes, estimated to be worth some £600 million. But added profits were not the only spur. The marketeers had identified 'up front' in the aircraft as an unrivalled shop window for British Airways among an influential and highly-discriminating group of purchasers who bought seats there. Colin Marshall was frank about the thinking behind the changes: 'There are no indications of major growth in the first-class market, so our objective is to take business from other airlines by offering the highest standard of passenger service in the world.'

To do this, the airline invested £24 million (changing business class had cost £25 million). The expectation was that this would add up to 20% to first-class sales over the following two years; a quarter of a million passengers a year were travelling first with BA when the changes were introduced. Main thrusts were redesigned interiors to the first-class cabin, improvements to the sleeper seats with which the cabins were already fitted, including tables which swivelled so that passengers could leave their seats even when the table had been laid, improved menus and the freedom to eat when the passenger – not the airline – dictated, a new wine list, and the introduction of what the airline claimed was the world's first individually-controlled video (the individual screens came up out of the armrests and the passengers chose what they wanted to watch from a selection of fifty video tapes carried on board each flight).

The two years of extensive research which BA carried out before introducing its new top-of-the-range product in spring 1989 showed that its first-class customer fell into two distinct categories – the 'patrician' and the 'achiever'. The patrician, the airline said, had established wealth, was relaxed, but had exacting standards, did not want to be over-pampered, and chose first class as a matter of course. The achiever was usually a self-made man who was more status-conscious, was a conspicuous consumer, sought recognition, and used first class as 'a signal of accomplishment'. Whether patrician or achiever, in the revamped BA de luxe cabins they sat on seats with 62 inches of legroom from the one in front, 20 inches wide, and which reclined to a position near the horizontal, walked on substantial woollen carpets which were changed every few weeks, and ate – off specially-designed Royal Doulton china – sybaritic meals with a choice of four main courses, including lobster with Welsh mussels in a Chablis sauce with mustard seed, and fresh Barbary-duck with truffled stuffing garnished with grapes and walnuts.

Life aboard BA's shuttle services was plainly never going to be as lush, but the airline's marketeers spent as much time – two years – teasing out the changes to this product as they did on first class. This time the launch was done in an instant garden created overnight in one of the airline's engineering hangars at Heathrow, with Members of Parliament and business leaders from the four shuttle terminals – Heathrow, Belfast, Glasgow and Edinburgh – invited to hear the story. The statistics were remarkable. Super Shuttle was, by 1989, carrying three and a half million passengers a year on the four routes on 30 000 scheduled flights, and several thousand unscheduled ones as the promise never to leave a passenger behind was honoured (forty-five back-ups had been flown on one particularly busy day). But although shuttle was such a galloping success, it created intense problems for BA in meeting its pledge: not only was it ferociously expensive in aircraft and manpower (keeping an airliner and its flight and crew standing by costs BA around £5000 an hour), but with the airways over Britain crowded at the morning and evening peaks (when shuttle is most heavily used by its mainly business clientele) good timekeeping was difficult.

There was a lack of air jetties on occasions at the Heathrow terminal, meaning that passengers had to board across the apron, while British Midland was snapping at BA's heels – which produced a sideswipe from Colin Marshall at the shuttle relaunch:

It is only because of Super Shuttle that others are able to operate at all. We fly at all hours, and in all weathers. They fly only at peak times, so offering a service that is less than comprehensive. And if their planes are grounded by the weather, or not sufficiently full, they simply cancel them and advise their passengers to switch to Super Shuttle, where we are happy to welcome them and serve them.

Lord King also took the opportunity to fire a salvo at British Midland and the group owning it, Michael Bishop's Airlines of Britain.

We are sick and tired of competitors who believe they should still be protected, and call foul every single time we seek to innovate with new products, new pricing policies and new route developments. What is it, in a free-enterprise unrestricted marketplace, which prompts the Airlines of Britain group to place formal objections in the path of every single new domestic route application made by British Airways? Why is it that they want to protect the monopolies they hold on so many air routes in this country?

There can be only one answer – they are frightened of commercial democracy. They do not like the idea of customers having the vote. We will not be put off by those who make big noises in public but who display their true nature by carping to the regulators. The market will, in the end, see through their tactics to confuse the issue of competition. Our job remains relatively simple – to provide the kind of style and scope of airline service, in the air and on the ground, that the consumer in Belfast, Edinburgh, Glasgow, London and Manchester legitimately demands. We are a willing seller. Only ensuring that our products are the most competitive in every respect will the customer be a willing buyer.

The main changes introduced on Super Shuttle routes from September 1989 – and they cost the airline £11 million this time – were two different types of travel, machines to issue tickets and boarding passes, and improved catering, with hot lunches and dinners on all routes except London–Manchester (where the airborne time was too short to serve anything but cold cuts). Passengers prepared to pay the full fare continued to be guaranteed a stand-by flight if the first section was full, and could arrive and check-in only ten minutes before departure. Those buying cheaper 'Savers' tickets were expected to book in advance. BA justified this policy by saying that most of these were leisure travellers and, 'with their more predictable travelling arrangements, they prefer the certainty of a prebooked seat to the "turn up and take off" facility that is so valuable to business travellers'.

With club, first class and shuttle 'branded', the marketeers went on to revamp Concorde, economy class and cargo, the intention being to apply the process throughout the airline's products. Just before he retired from the airline, Jim Harris explained the thinking behind this trend:

What airlines sell is a commodity, and this is particularly true of the package tour. Ask most people on packages what airline they are flying with and they do not know. This can be translated to the supermarket situation, where the big companies ask the manufacturers to produce goods and then put their own labels on them – Tesco and Sainsbury have their own champagne. This could happen in our service industry, with the retailer having control of the brand and the airline becoming the egg in the sandwich.

British Airways feels strongly that it cannot get into that position. It really cannot afford not to be in control of its own distribution system. Through branding, it can create a strong difference between itself and its competitors, and BA can make sure that the public asks for BA. After all, there are plenty of different hamburgers, but nobody can buy a McDonald's hamburger anywhere but McDonald's.

BA will now go anywhere to find people with experience of being brand managers, because you are not going to find them in the service industries.

And marketing's role for the future?

The marketeers want to see British Airways as a quality airline, reliable and very warm – one that people are prepared to pay a premium to fly with providing it gives them service. British Airways will have its white sales, but it will also provide the best standards of service because that is what the management believes people want in the global market.

Finding out what customers really want from the airlines is a matter for surveys among passengers, of sifting through their letters of complaint and, occasionally, commendation. Going out to seek criticism is not a common industry trait. British Airways was therefore cracking a mould when it erected video booths at Heathrow and Gatwick airports in which unhappy customers who had been bumped, or subjected to other aviation indignities, could give management a piece of their mind, and also when it set up a conference at a centre near Windsor in the spring of 1989, inviting some of its most vocal regulars to spend a day parading their grouses. Some 150 arrived at the centre, all of them big spenders across the whole range of services which BA provides, from Concorde to shuttle. There to meet them, with only the faintest quiver of a lip visible here and there, were fifty of the airline's top managers.

The attendees at this customer forum had been exhorted to be frank, but in the early skirmishing the complaints were of a fairly minor nature – the taste of the coffee served on board, the temperature of the wines. Languages spoken, or rather not spoken, by BA staff was another perennial, quickly raised. 'One area where your airline falls far short of any other European airline is in the question of languages', one delegate told the assembled marketeers and other assorted management people. 'Swissair and Air France give announcements in two languages. BA sometimes struggles to give them in one.' Mike Batt, Head of Brand Management, pointed out that Britain as a nation was hardly renowned for its linguistic ability but ethnic staff had been introduced on the long-haul routes, while in Europe 'we are improving'. BA was investing in language laboratories, and was looking at pay structures to give incentives to those with languages. Smoking on board turned out to be a hot subject and another delegate thought BA should 'have the guts' to ban it on flights of under two hours' duration. Batt pointed out that smoking had already been banned on domestic flights, adding, 'It is coming. We are looking at the future route by route. We are told that on services to and from Istanbul, Madrid and Rome, it is a no no. With 23 million customers, they are never going to want the same.' Inevitably in-flight food came in for a drubbing. One lady delegate said she was fed up with the meal on the tray on the Brussels route: 'No account is taken of time of day, and the vegetarian meal would not sustain anybody except a rabbit.'

During the day, the conference broke up into a series of small discussion groups, one of which debated which class of travel people flew long-haul if they were expected to arrive bushy-tailed. Mike Batt replied, 'There are Trojans who go straight into meetings after eleven hours in an economy seat, but there are also other managers who say they need recuperation time. In the case of BA staff travelling on duty, if they come back first-class and they land at 7.30 am, they are in the office at 8.30 am. If they come back economy, I would not be justified in having them in the office by that time.' 'What is BA doing to meet the extremely good service by Virgin Atlantic out of Gatwick?', another delegate wanted to know. Liam Strong, Marketing Director: 'We agree that Richard Branson is doing an incredible job on a small scale, and we welcome any competition which prevents us being complacent. But we do not believe that Branson is performing better than BA.' Sir Colin Marshall added, 'We did have a pretty awful performance out of Gatwick in 1988. We are not proud of it, and we have been working hard to stop it happening again.' Was the cost of travel for BA executives on duty debited to their profit centres, and if not why not, another attendee inquired. David Burnside, Director of Public Affairs, replied, 'There are long, historic reasons for staff travel, and there are different categories within the airline for staff travelling on duty. In general, from Lord King across the board, senior management will be downgraded and offloaded. We do not put off commercial passengers because staff are travelling on duty.'

Corporate soul-baring in this vein continued throughout the conference, at the end of which most of the marketeers present said they saw their airline in a new light. Summing up, Colin Marshall said that there was a time when the airline industry was what he called 'a closed and comfortable club,' where nobody felt that they had to work that hard and where events moved in their own leisurely time frames. 'Those days', he added uncompromisingly, 'are now gone for ever.'

CHAPTER SEVEN

THE ENGINEERS: PUTTING IT ALL TOGETHER

Buying a new armchair for the home is a reasonably straightforward business. You start by looking at a brochure, then you go to view the product in a local store; you walk round it, sit in it, stretch your legs for a few moments. If you are happy you sign a cheque, and in a few days or weeks a van delivers the new acquisition to your door.

British Airways bought a new chair for the club-class cabins of its long-haul airliners, but in the airline's case the selection procedure was a touch more complicated than the domestic scenario outlined above. Airline seats differ from the domestic variety in that not only do they have to be liked by those who sit in them – and a BA seat can be 'home' to a passenger for anything up to a day and a half if he or she is flying from London to Australia – they have to satisfy rigid engineering and safety standards. In the case of a sudden deceleration of the aircraft they must withstand forces up to sixteen times that of gravity; the material in which they are covered must keep fire from reaching the interior foam long enough to allow the occupant to escape before being overcome by poisonous fumes; they must be easy to keep clean and inviting-looking, despite heavy wear (they will, the airline hopes, be occupied for most of their life); and the mechanical systems with which they are packed – reclining back, extendable footrest, reading-light control, cabin-crew call button, plug-in video and audio systems – have to be reliable, and simple to maintain.

Airline seats are, in fact, a precision engineering job, and this was why BA's engineering staff played such an important role in the choice of the new ones which went into the B747 and TriStar cabins when Club World was launched at the beginning of 1988. Such problems are the bread and butter of the development engineers who form a small group within BA's total complement of 7000 engineering workers. As one of them said, 'Everybody is an expert when it comes to seats'; so the airline set up a small action group, which included marketing, purchasing and operations, as well as engineering, to vet the products which were on offer by the specialist aerospace seat manufacturers.

BA funded five such companies, four from Britain, one from France, to design and produce a sample pair of seats, telling each of them, 'We want the best that you can make.' When the five pairs arrived, the airline tested them in the only true way – by putting bottoms on them. Some 600 of BA's regular travellers were invited along at weekends to various hotels near Heathrow to lounge in the contenders for an hour, their reactions being carefully noted by a team of researchers both before and after they sat down. Then a group of BA employees who normally fly club class on duty tried the seats out on an all-night basis. The airline had the seats installed in hotel bedrooms for this test, and to make sure that there was no cheating had the beds taken out.

Ergonomists, scientists who specialise in fitting the human body into different working environments, were employed to look at the competing seats, devoid of any emotion. These 'seat clinics', as BA called them, resulted in hefty reports which, when analysed, showed one of the five a clear winner. BA duly ordered 2000 seats from this one manufacturer; as they cost somewhere between £1000 and £2500 each – the airline insists on being vague about the real figure for competitive commercial reasons – it was an order to be cherished. The development engineer commented, 'Our engineering judgement had been that it was better to wait for a better seat, and the seat which this company produced proved us right. It was certainly far better than anything that was on the market already.'

The end-product in this case was highly visible to BA's fare-paying customers, but 95% of the work of the airline's engineers goes on behind the scenes, on a round-the-clock basis. Theirs is an exacting task, for their charges, BA's fleet of 200 airliners, the engines that power them, and the multitude of highly complicated systems which are built into them, operate in a hostile environment in which the spectre of the force of gravity is always lurking. Keeping an airline flying safely, and on time, is not a case of waiting until mechanical trouble shows itself and then charging in to do running repairs. Rather is it a case of preventive maintenance, with each airliner having its own computerised case papers, and bookings earmarked into the maintenance base years in advance for a running series of checks, overhauls and modifications which never end during a lifetime, between the manufacturer and the scrap merchant, of twenty years or more.

Entrance into this highly-skilled world is far from easy. There are high academic hurdles to be cleared, and lengthy trade apprenticeships to be completed, before any young man or woman can hope to lay hands upon one of BA's machines. The tiros emerge from their schools with O-levels or the equivalent in subjects such as mathematics, English and science, and if they impress the airline sufficiently are selected for its apprenticeship scheme. In common with many other British companies, BA operates an attainment-based scheme rather than a time-served system. The apprenticeship lasts three years but those who stay the course emerge simply as skilled trades-men, without the special qualifications which are required to work on aircraft on their own and without supervision. BA then takes them through a series of specialised training courses involving classroom work, firstly in the basic knowledge associated with aircraft and their systems, and then on specific courses related to aircraft types and their particular systems. It is only after they have completed those courses that they qualify for licences. A very good candidate could be a certified lead tradesman five years after starting his apprenticeship; if he is very, very good, he could take six months off that. Only at that stage can he begin to work on an aircraft and sign for work which he has done. When he signs, he is legally responsible for that work.

In an average year BA will take on fifty engineering apprentices. Early in his or her career with the airline, each will be asked to decide whether they want to specialise on engines, airframes, or aviation electronics. Their initial training is at engineering schools outside BA, after which they attend the airline's own training centre at Cranebank, on the edge of Heathrow airport. On-the-job training in aeronautical skills comes in BA's own hangars. Training for specific licences is done in the airline's own engineering training department, where a staff of 125 pass on their specialised knowledge. These specialists also teach engineering staff from other airlines; there are usually around 300 of these learning from BA at any one time.

Aviation engineering gets into the blood, and those who join BA in this department often stay for a long time: there are some who have been with the airline, and its predecessors, for forty years. Pride in the job is there, and no opportunity is lost by management to promote it further. Good house-keeping awards were instituted by Alistair Cumming, BA's Engineering Director, so that teams of workers can suddenly find themselves the recipients of awards worth as much as £150 apiece for keeping their work stations cleaner and tidier than others. Awards for inventive ideas that will save the airline time and money can run into thousands of pounds.

It is hardly surprising that there is an accent on keeping engineering efficient and cost-effective, for the expenditure in this sector is formidable. The airline's annual bill for the 400 000 spare parts which it uses comes to £110 million; a tyre for a Boeing 747 main wheel costs £300, a main landing-gear for the same aircraft £600 000, a similar type of assembly for a Concorde over £1 million. It goes without saying that every price increase sought by BA's 8000 suppliers is resisted, monitored and investigated.

BA also sets out to market its engineering services as a way of generating income. The engineering department has a special unit established to spread the message around the world industry, and has found it beneficial to this drive to take stand space at recent international air shows such as Farnborough and Le Bourget, Paris. This business for other airliner operators (known as third-party work) now brings BA over £60 million worth of revenue a year. These third-party clients range from airlines with which BA competes fiercely in the marketplace to the flying palaces of Arab princes, with their double beds, gold-plated seat-belt buckles and bathroom taps, perches for falcons, and indicators let into the ceiling which always point to the holy city of Mecca, wherever the aircraft might be flying in the world. BA has around 100 third-party customers on its books, and it is not only whole aircraft which are contracted. Engine overhaul for others is carried out at Heathrow, and at BA's specialist engine-overhaul base at Treforest, South Wales; undercarriages come in for refurbishment for some of the big North American carriers; single cockpit instruments arrive for attention from remote parts of the globe, property of airlines you would be hard pressed to find in the most detailed aviation reference books.

The engineering department treats them all the same, returning battered and grimy pieces of equipment shiny as new, checked and rechecked. BA's third-party work may not be the cheapest in the world, but its delivery-on-time reputation is excellent, while the immense facilities and human expertise which it can muster are impressive. It has time to spare to work for others because of improvements in productivity introduced in recent years. Much of the heavy maintenance work on the aircraft is now scheduled for the winter months, so that more aircraft are available for flying during the peak summer months. This means that there is spare capacity in the workshops in the summer, and the drive to capture outside contracts for this period intensifies.

BA's engineering managers see third-party work not only as a way of helping to maximise the airline's massive capital investment in its buildings, plant and manpower, but as a shop-window for the airline and its capabilities. They also see such work as fine-tuning BA skills, because the contracts are highly demanding from the point of view of quality, and BA's workers know that they are having to satisfy critical outsiders as well as themselves. One golden rule is that no outside work is ever taken on if it would cut across work on BA's own fleet; but the engineers like the challenge of 'taking in somebody else's washing', and the story is recalled around the base of how a group which had finished a job on a rival airline's BAC 1–11 early was found filling in time by giving the aircraft a hand polish, 'just to impress the others'.

Spare time is rare. As mentioned earlier, every BA airliner has its future maintenance life charted in detail from the moment that it enters the fleet, while its history, and that of the thousands of parts inside it, are meticulously logged on computerised records. Enforced by the Civil Aviation

Authority (CAA), which has inspectors permanently on site, a series of checks, becoming progressively bigger, are laid down for each aircraft type, depending on the number of flight-hours the aircraft has completed. Each 747 in BA's fleet has, for instance, 3.67 engineering man-hours devoted to it before each take-off, and 9.77 man-hours daily. Major servicing begins after 850 flying hours, when 534 man-hours are expended on it, increasing to no fewer than 26 204 man-hours, or twenty-four days of work, after four years of flying.

The 3.67 man-hours on the airport apron are carried out in that hectic period while a 747 is being emptied and cleaned from one flight, and refuelled and revictualled for the next. Tasks range from such simple matters as replacing a dead light bulb to the removal of magnetic-chip detectors from the engines. These are plugs which lie in the engine-oil system and pick up tell-tale metal particles which indicate to the trained eye that an engine may need attention; BA inspects around 63 000 of these every year. Today's engineers are helped by the fact that modern airliners have their own built-in test equipment which indicates what has gone wrong and its location. Black boxes going 'on the blink' can be unplugged and a replacement plugged in. The generator on a Viscount airliner consisted of eighty parts, but today's equivalent is contained in two easily-removable units. The earliest automatic-landing system on a Trident airliner was driven by twenty-seven units; on BA's 757s today, that number has reduced to three.

There are some parts of an airliner which it is impossible to inspect closely with the naked eye without taking the airliner to pieces, an expensive and time-consuming job which would also reduce the hours it spends in the air earning money. To solve this problem, BA has built up a non-destructive testing department, the high technology of which has many similarities with that found in hospitals. The analogy is sound, for the airline's specialist engineers in the NDT department are, like hospital doctors, looking inside their 'patients' for signs of systems malfunction, and like hospital doctors they use devices such as X-rays, ultrasonic sound-waves, and heat detection. What they are looking for as they probe and scan are the minute maladies peculiar to aircraft however well they are maintained — cracking of the airframe and engines, corrosion, which can be caused by rainwater seeping in, by spillage from the toilets, even by fruit juices and other liquids slopped in the galleys.

Once again BA sells its specialised knowledge and services in NDT to other airlines and aircraft operators. One of the department's specialities is the examination of airliner undercarriage wheels, items which take a tremendous hammering as they settle 300 tons of Boeing 747 on to concrete runways. BA inspects fifty wheels every working day; each joins a queue on a roller-bed to take a turn on a BA-designed and developed machine which picks it up, spins it on a device like the turntable of a record player, and then sends into it, through a probe, an eddy current which shows up the slightest imperfection on a printed tape. Flaws embedded deep inside metal can also be identified by passing sound-waves as high-frequency mechanical vibrations into the object; the waves which return are shown on cathode-ray tubes, and early signs of trouble are identified by the skilled eyes of the NDT technicians. BA has borrowed here from the armed forces, the procedure being similar to that used by ships to detect submarines by bouncing sound-waves back off the metal hull.

Penetrating dyes are used to show up imperfections in metal surfaces. Since defects disrupt magnetic paths, magnetism is applied, the blemishes revealing themselves when special inks are painted on. Thermography 'reads' changes of temperature in the metal and other materials which make up an aircraft; this is particularly useful in identifying places on an airframe which are allowing water to leak in, for water, frozen at the altitudes at which an airliner flies, remains cold long after landing and reveals itself on the thermographic image as a dark patch. (The same process is used in hospitals for the treatment of cancer, and by rescue services to locate trapped people by homing on the heat radiated by their bodies.) The equipment used by BA is able to detect temperature changes as small as one-tenth of a degree centigrade.

NDT procedures are far from cheap. A roll of the X-ray film which BA uses to see inside the structures of its airliners costs £500, and the annual bill for such film comes to around £75 000. BA has its own X-ray laboratory; to guard against radiation hazards, it is encased in concrete 27 inches thick and its doors are lined with lead. The engineers who take the pictures work from outside and wear film badges to make sure that they are not receiving more than the safe dosage. Gamma rays are used to probe the remote insides of jet engines; here the regulations, made under Act of Parliament, are even stricter. Geiger counters are used to measure safety levels, while the isotope – just $1\frac{1}{2}$ mm. long – is kept locked away when not in use and can only be obtained by certain members of the engineering staff, who have to sign for it.

The airline processes its own X-ray film at its base, using automatic equipment; finished pictures can be ready ten minutes after the shots have been taken. Mobile equipment is on hand for assignments abroad. Interpreting the results is a skilled business, and it takes a year and a half to build up the total expertise required – four years to master all the NDT techniques. Experienced technicians are able to differentiate between sixteen shades of grey on an X-ray plate, and can point out the minutest hair-line crack, which would totally escape the eye of layman but which could be the start of something much more serious. The radiographs which are pored over are the actual size of the part of the airliner which has been photographed. After the inspection the plates are filed in a library, to be brought out when that same airliner next comes in for inspection and compared with the pictures taken then.

For the future, BA has been looking at the possibility of fixing a series of microphones to the airframes of airliners to detect changes in the noise 'signature' produced while the aircraft are flying; and at neutron radiography, a process which can look through a brick wall and pick out a milk bottle standing on the other side – used by BA, it could peer at the state of the oil in a jet engine, without the engine getting in the way.

BA's engineers, used to dealing with the basic aerospace metals – aluminium alloy, steel, titanium – have to remain flexible in their approach, ready to deal with new materials as they come along. Composites, such as fibreglass, carbon fibre and Kevlar, are forming increasingly large proportions of aircraft structures. They are light and strong, but they require new techniques for upkeep and repair. Radomes – the nose cone of an airliner which covers the swivelling radar dish inside – are made of composites because of their non-reflective properties; but because of their position at the very front of the aircraft they do come in for damage, particularly when the flight has been through heavy rain or a hailstorm. BA now has specialists in its fibreglass shop who are experts in removing the dents and sanding radomes down to good-as-new condition, work that is well worthwhile when a radome on a Boeing 747 costs £25 000 while one on a Concorde works out at £1 million.

Concorde, in fact, poses particular engineering problems, and BA has a special team of 300 engineers who look after its fleet of seven racehorses of the sky. The racehorse simile is apt, for while Concorde is a thoroughbred which is faster than all the others, she also needs an above-average amount of looking after and can be temperamental at times. The Concorde team, some of whom also work on Boeing 757s, form a close-knit 'family' who have developed strong loyalties to their supersonic charges, and an individual knowledge of each particular aircraft and the myriad parts of which it is made.

Some 50% of BA's Concorde engineers have worked with the airliner since it entered service in 1976; the experience of others goes back even further. They are the ones who joined the airline after being involved with British Aerospace in the long development programme of the Anglo-French supersonic, a programme which went on for seven years before the aircraft was cleared to carry passengers. There is something special about being involved in Concorde maintenance; it is almost like being a member of a rather exclusive club, where everybody knows everybody else, and where all concerned are prepared to join in and talk over problems. And like every aircraft ever built Concorde does have its problems, although they are somewhat different from those which are thrown up by the subsonic airliner fleet.

The origins of Concorde go back to the 1960s, so that although it has some systems which are right up with the times – like partial fly-by-wire, in which commands from the flight-deck to the moving surfaces are signalled electronically rather than mechanically, and computer-controlled doors to the engine intakes to control the airflow at various speeds – much of the design of the aircraft is now quite old. The flight-deck, for instance, is out-moded by today's 'glass cockpit' on BA's 757s, 767s and latest 747s, which are packed with colour cathode-ray tubes bearing the instrumentation, rather than electromechanical dials; but updating it would be a lengthy and ruinously expensive job, and would put the aircraft on the ground for too long.

Keeping Concorde's systems in good shape provides a daily challenge for its technological 'minders'. The Rolls-Royce–Snecma Olympus 593 engines have to have their airflow controlled because they would be unable to digest air coming at them at supersonic speeds. The air is slowed down through the use of what the industry calls 'barn doors', computer-controlled, with a pair of computers for each intake so that there are eight boxes in all, with all their wiring. These are large first-generation devices. If their design was to be redone today the boxes would, given the galloping pace of microchip technology, all go into one small computer.

Concorde is also the only civil airliner in the world which expands by some ten inches during supersonic flight, contracting to its normal length when it returns to the ground. Flying at 1350 mph its airframe is subject to intense friction, and there is a probe on the nose which sends signals to the engines to slow down if there is a danger of safe speed being exceeded. The designers got it absolutely right in fabricating Concorde from a special aluminium alloy, developed for jet engines, which always resumes its original shape; but even this would begin to melt if the aircraft went too fast.

The BA engineers also have to be conversant with Concorde's pioneering braking system, in which steel was replaced by carbon fibre to give both lightness and the greater stopping power required for the higher speeds at which the aircraft takes off and lands. Concorde also led the industry in having a system which warns the crew, with a light in the cockpit, if a tyre has suffered damage during taxying. It also has, of course, its unique 'droop snoot', its long nose which is lowered for take-off and landing to give the flight-deck crew of two pilots and flight engineer a better view of the runway. Glass said to be the toughest in the world was specially developed for the visor to withstand the impact of birds at high speeds.

Then the BA engineers have to grapple with Concorde's complicated fuel system – thirteen tanks, including one in the tail (compared with five in a 747). During flight, fuel is pumped between them as a way of adjusting the aircraft's centre of gravity. As a result Concorde has a large number of fuel pumps, valves and gauges, which need to be checked and occasionally replaced. Its hydraulics also work at higher pressure than those of subsonic airliners, which means that a careful watch has to be kept on the system's many seals; its hydraulic fluid, developed specially to resist high temperatures, is very expensive.

The men whose speciality is the supersonic bird understand intimately all these unusual features and the problems which they can throw up. Many of these features have led to spin-offs in aerospace and other industries. Fly-by-wire is in the A320 150-seat airliner, which BA took into its fleet in early 1988; carbon brakes are gradually becoming standard on new military and civil aircraft designs, and are fitted to Formula One racing cars; the toughened glass which was developed for the droop snoot has found its way into the windscreens of family saloons.

The pilots and flight engineers who fly BA's Concordes also play their part in the enormous engineering effort which goes into the supersonic aircraft, feeding back how each aircraft performs in flight, identifying possible snags. The rapport between flight and ground crews remains immense, and frequently on first-name terms. One Concorde captain said,

> You can't run away from the fact that you are flying an aircraft that does a lot of things that other aircraft do not do. If you did not have faith in the engineers, you would be sitting on the edge of your seat the whole time. But we know that the aircraft are always presented to us for service in first-class condition, and that underlying faith in the whole maintenance procedure is shared by all our flight crews.

The change of BA's 'image' which came in early 1985 placed engineering under tremendous pressure. There were 150 airliners to be repainted in the new colours and refurbished inside. The work on the twenty-eight Boeing 747s then in the fleet, which included new seats, galleys and toilets, constituted, at £60 million, probably the most expensive facelift in the history of civil aviation. A similar job on the TriStar fleet cost some £30 million. The work was in phases, coded Sunset 1, 2 and 3. Bigger overhead bins were fitted for passengers' carry-on baggage; sidewall panels were replaced with new ones in the latest BA colours; outmoded super-eight in-flight film systems were taken out and the latest video systems put in. Sunset 2, under which, to spread the load, some of the work was sent to the big airline engineering company Haeco in Hong Kong, saw eight old galleys in each aircraft discarded in favour of fourteen new ones, all to BA's ACE design, which had been carefully drawn up so that various trolleys and other equipment used on board would fit into any of the types of aircraft operated by the airline.

Among the new toilet units fitted were several larger ones specifically designed for use by disabled people. Miles of new carpet were laid. Bulkheads were re-covered in new materials in the new corporate livery,

with those in the first-class section covered in grey leather. Improved facilities for coats and suit-bags were installed. Also, under the Sunset programme, seats in first and club classes were re-covered in new fabrics, with
the leg-rests in first fitted with a mechanism to extend them at the touch of a
button. Economy-class cabins had new seats – somebody in BA worked out
that if all the seats which were being shipped out to Haeco for installation in
the 747s were laid side by side, they would stretch for two miles, or almost
as long as the runways at Heathrow.

Refurbishing work on the TriStars was subcontracted out to the aircraft
engineering company Marshall, of Cambridge, and included the moving of
the galleys from the belly hold, from where they were linked to the main
deck by elevators, up to the main deck, so leaving room below for an
additional eight freight containers. TriStars too were fitted with new
seating, bulkheads, carpets, galleys, toilets and baggage storage. In both
747s and TriStars the layout of the cabins was changed to give a better
environment for passengers and crews. At the same time each aircraft was
given a major check which virtually entailed a total taking apart. To the
layman visiting the BA engineering base on such occasions, all looked chaos
as overalled technicians swarmed over, under and through the stranded
leviathan, its bulk shrouded inside one of BA's gigantic movable docks; it
was easy to despair of it ever all going back together again. But every move
in such operations is predetermined by manufacturer, airline, and aviation
authority, and after three weeks of intensive engineering attention each
'jumbo' rolled out as good as – if not better than – new, and ready to go back
into revenue-producing service.

Just painting a 747 is a major operation; the paint which is stripped off
weighs 450 pounds, but before that the airframe is prewashed by BA's
Chemical Cleaning Unit, and all areas which must not be touched by paint
stripper – including the windows, surfaces made of fibreglass, engines, and
undercarriage – are masked, using yards and yards of paper and sticky tape.
Stripping fluid sprayed on to the aircraft causes the old paint to go soft and
begin to run, with an effect which is like something out of a *Quatermass*
science fiction film. High-pressure jets and hand-scraping remove the mess,
but then the hard part begins, the rubbing down of the remainder by hand.
Edge stripping follows, a delicate operation which removes the paint right
up to the point where vulnerable surfaces, such as windows, join the metal.
When all the paint has finally gone the bare metal is given a shampoo and
rinse in water; then the maskings over the non-metallic areas are removed,
the fibreglass is rubbed down by hand, and there is a further shampoo and
rinse. Seals between skin-panel joints which might have been damaged during the stripping process are then repaired, and it is at that point that the
aircraft is ready for its new paint job.

A coat of acid anodising fluid is put on first, followed by a layer of epoxy-

Two BA engineers at work on a Rolls-Royce RB211 engine.

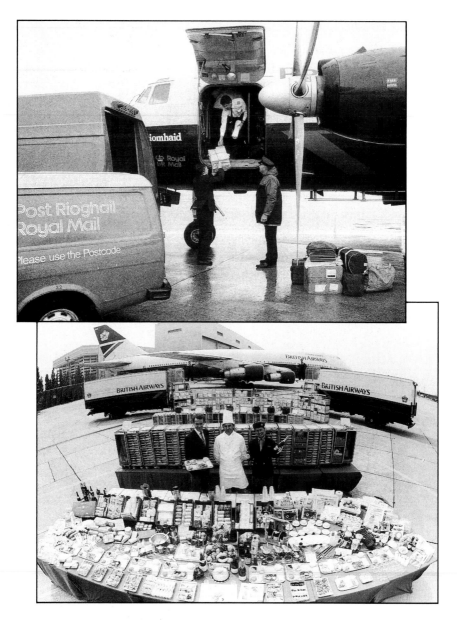

Above As a result of the 1981 management/union agreement BA staff in the Highlands Division became 'multi-functional'. Here a pilot helps unload a BA 748 'Budgie' at Benbecula, in the Western Isles, after the morning flight from Glasgow.
Below Some 36 000 items, from mustard pots to blankets, fresh fruit to newspapers, brandy to first-aid kits, go on to every 747. Keeping track of these items, and making certain that the right numbers are loaded, is one of the many jobs done by computer.

Training then and now. *Above* The latest piece of BA training hardware is this 747-400 simulator. Housed at the training complex at Cranebank, near Heathrow, this machine replicates a 'jumbo jet' flight right down to bumps in the runway concrete and the noise of the engines and gives 150 degrees of continuous horizontal vision. *Below* An early Link trainer used extensively by BEA in the immediate post-war years.

Opposite top A 'green from the tower' – or in this case, a caravan at the end of the runway, was the signal for BEA take-offs in the early post-war years. *Below* The control tower, Northolt 1948, shows the basic equipment required for the slow airliners in operation then. *This page* Today's air traffic controllers backed by computers and high-definition radars are struggling to keep pace with increasing air traffic. This is the visual control tower at Heathrow, the world's busiest international airport.
The diagram behind shows part of the Jeppesen high altitude *en route* chart covering southern England.

BA's advertising campaigns ranged from the whimsical to the punning, but best remembered for its impact was Manhattan landing, designed to bring home the strength of the airline's traffic across the North Atlantic.

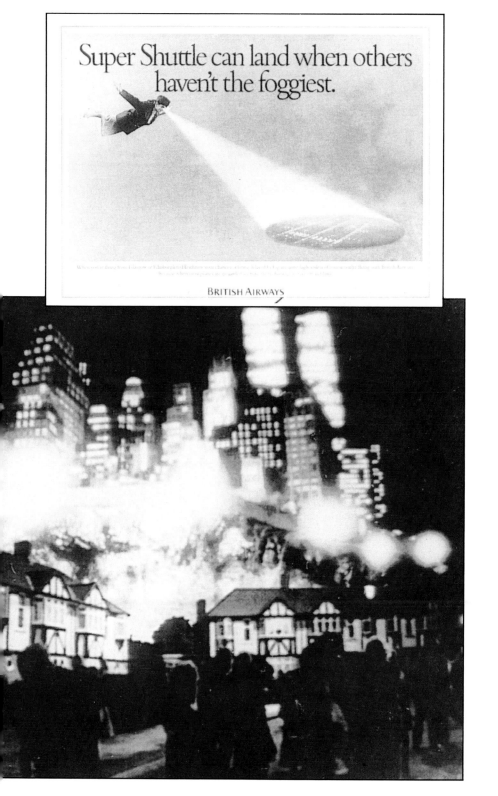

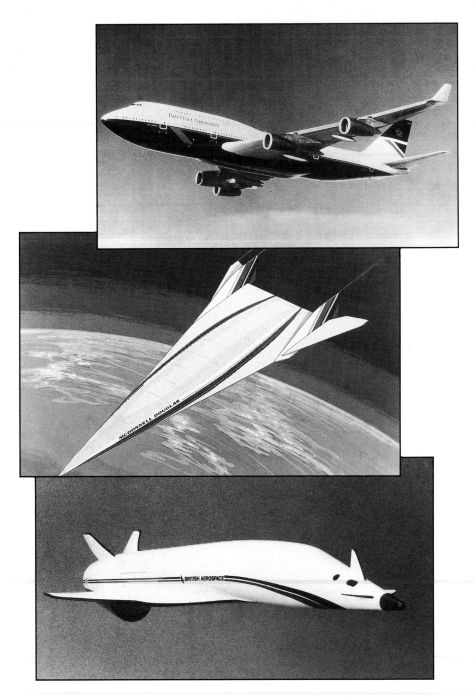

Top Today's Boeing 747–400 bears little resemblance to the first 'jumbo' produced in Seattle in 1968. It will almost certainly still be flying with BA in 2001. *Centre* The conceptual design of a McDonnell Douglas hypersonic airliner, to become a reality would require multi-million dollar investment. *Below* The British Hotol, a space vehicle using conventional airport facilities, could be a civil transport for the distant future.

resin primer, providing both protection and a key for the finishing coat. Then come two final coats of paint, starting with the grey fuselage top, and then the midnight blue on the tail fin, lower fuselage, and engines. When the main paint is on, more wrappings and maskings are applied and the detailed work starts. BA's red speedwing stripe is sprayed right down either side of the fuselage; the coat of arms, with its lion and unicorn heraldic beasts and its motto, 'To Fly To Serve', is applied carefully to the tail fin; dozens of letters and numbers, large and small, are either stencilled or stuck on to the body and wings. Concorde gets special treatment, an all-white colour scheme of her own – apart from the coat of arms, the speedwing stripe, and the blue and red quartered flag on the tail fin – so that it reflects the heat which it builds up as it streaks along at over twice the speed of sound at almost 60 000 feet.

All of this work is carried out in a specially-equipped paint hangar at BA's Heathrow engineering base. The painters go aloft (the tip of a Boeing 747's tail is 65 feet above the ground) on mobile platforms, to which they are harnessed for safety's sake, and for some of the painting processes wear filtered air-masks fed from a special air supply. The platforms are fitted with inertia-reel escape harnesses to allow the painters to reach the ground safely if anything were to go wrong.

Why paint at all, the engineers are sometimes asked? Why not leave the airliners in their pristine, bright aluminium construction? They are good questions, considering that BA uses up 933 litres of high-quality paint to cover a 747, sufficient to spray ninety family motor cars. The answer is that an airliner left in its basic metal would quickly corrode, both from the effects of the weather which it flies through and from the de-icing fluid which is sprayed over it in cold weather. A good and solid coating of paint, despite the weight penalty it imposes, will also save fuel, as it enables the airliner to slip more smoothly through the air, so reducing the drag factor.

Just occasionally BA's engineers face the melancholy but challenging task of putting back together an aircraft which has been damaged in an accident. The airline has one man designated Aircraft Recovery Specialist, and he keeps a bag packed at home ready to fly off to any part of the world at a moment's notice. John McLeod was the person in this particular hot seat on 6 May 1986. He had just returned home at 7 pm, looking forward to a quiet weekend, when he was rung by engineering control to say that an RAF TriStar, a type which BA maintains under third-party contract, had made a particularly heavy landing at RAF Brize Norton, Oxfordshire.

Two hours later he was at Brize, making a first assessment of a sorry sight. The port undercarriage was bent out of the vertical. Fuel running from the port rear spar, and damage to piping and cables, indicated that the spar had been fractured. There was a tear and buckling in the port wing skin, and the port wing had assumed what was drily noted by the BA people as 'an overall twist'. The force with which the aircraft had made contact with the ground was also evident inside the cabin, with roof panels lying on the seats and toilet doors off their hinges. The risk of moving an aircraft in such a state is well known, so it was decided to remove all the fuel, and review the situation at dawn the following day.

The next morning the stricken TriStar was towed gingerly off the runway, where it had come to rest, to the hangar apron. A BA recovery team which had arrived set about lightening the aircraft by removing its engines and cabin furnishings. The TriStar was then moved into a hangar, but because of its size its tail stuck out through the doors – a problem which was solved when the airline brought in the scaffolding firm SGB to erect a box which encased the tail completely. One hundred tons of scaffold tubes were used, and the resulting structure was stressed to withstand winds of up to 70 mph. BA's damage survey was completed by 24 June and the go-ahead was given for the repair. Order sheets for over 2000 items were passed to BA's Line Spares Section; many of them had to be ordered direct from Lockheed in Burbank, California, as they were structural. In some cases they were designed specifically for the repair job.

As BA engineering said afterwards, 'The task that lay ahead at that stage was not for faint-hearted aircraft engineers. It's one thing to build an aero-plane like a TriStar from scratch, but it's quite another, and in many ways more difficult, to carry out major structural repairs.' Cutting out damaged parts was a task calling for skill, delicacy and strength. The top-skin plank of the wing, three-eights of an inch thick, had to be removed, the rear spar, spar caps and web between the undercarriage and centre torque box cut out, as were the inner-wing tank ribs. Numerous stringers, brackets, items of plumbing and wiring had to be removed. Due to distortion, some of the stringers had to be parted from the aircraft by the use of winches, while the port undercarriage only surrendered after a long struggle, and a bit of per-suasion with a 14-pound sledgehammer.

TriStars had gone out of production some years earlier, so that there were long lead times on some of the structural items which were needed. BA engineering executives and senior RAF officers flew out to Burbank to discuss the problem with Lockheed, returning with delivery promises. Meanwhile the team at Brize were repairing trailing edges, forward spars and wing ribs. The work was then suspended for a time for the arrival of parts from the United States, the team resuming on 10 October, and giving a completion date of 16 February 1987. The new spar section arrived, fol-lowed by stringers, wing panels, and rib sections. By this stage, the BA team were installing one-off, undrilled components costing thousands of pounds, a procedure calling for high degrees of skill, often in areas of the aircraft where there was very limited access.

By now the number of parts ordered has passed the 2500 mark, and hundreds of parts had been fabricated by the BA men on site. Thousands of fasteners of over 800 different types and lengths were used. One of the trickiest and most bruising jobs was assembling the ribs inside the wing fuel tank, where progress was limited by the number of men who could work at one time in the confined space. A visitor from the Ministry of Defence asked the crew how long they had been working in such a confined area. The reply came, 'Eight to twelve.' 'Well,' said the MoD man, 'that's not a bad working day.' He withdrew the observation hastily when it was pointed out that the working day was in fact eight in the morning until 12 midnight.

Structural work was complete by December, and the job of sealing the fuel tanks and installing some 100 internal fuel pipes began. Fuel-leak checks showed no drips from the repaired wing, but the starboard side, after lying dry for seven months, leaked. BA's engineers opened it up, and resealed it. Engines, undercarriages and flaps were reinstalled, plumbing and wiring snaked back into place. The passenger cabin was given a facelift, with extensive rewiring in places. Functional checks, undercarriage retractions, flaps and aileron rigging all went to plan, and by 6 February the aircraft was pronounced free of defects. Rebirth had happened exactly nine months after the accident. Compass swings and engine runs followed. On 15 February the RAF took the TriStar up for a demanding test flight, and on the following day, exactly as forecast six months previously, Alistair Cumming, BA's Director of Engineering, handed it back in a formal ceremony to the RAF.

The 800 different types of fasteners used in the TriStar repair came from British Airways' engineering spares holding, which runs to hundreds of thousands of parts worth, in all, in the region of £300 million. These are stored at sixty locations in Britain, and at many more of the overseas stations, where the airline has its own engineers resident. Keeping track of such an enormous and complicated inventory could be an expensive nightmare, but most of the worry and guesswork was taken out in 1987 when the airline went over to what it claims is the industry's most advanced computer inventory-control system in the world. Called TIME, total inventory management for engineering, it handles 170 000 transactions a day, using double-entry control, light pens, and bar-coding.

Every request for a part is identified in the TIME system by the 'giver' despatching the part, the receiver ordering the part, and a record of the part itself. The information is obtained from the bar-coding, which is similar to the system at supermarket check-outs, and is entered into TIME through the light pens. TIME took three years to set up. During this period new computer programmes were developed, every spare part in the airline's massive inventory was bar-coded, 340 double-entry light-pen work stations, and over 700 colour visual display units, with light-pen attachments, were introduced in engineering locations at Heathrow, Gatwick, Manchester and Glasgow, and a training programme for 6000 engineers was completed. BA worked out that TIME needed the equivalent of 100 man-years of work to develop, plan and implement. It was estimated that the system would save the airline £30 million over the first four years after its introduction, largely because it would produce a dramatic improvement in stock accuracy on quantity. Before TIME was introduced, engineering achieved about 55% accuracy. If a stock record said that there were, for instance, 100 of a certain part in stock, the chance of there being exactly 100 was only 55% – or a 45% chance of the quantity being wrong. TIME was designed to achieve a stock accuracy of better than 95%.

CHAPTER EIGHT

ACQUIRING AIRLINERS:
THE BIG CONUNDRUM

On a brilliantly sunny afternoon in late July 1989, two brand-new Boeing 747–400 airliners in the livery of British Airways were lined up nose-to-nose at Boeing Field, Seattle, in the north-west corner of the United States. The red carpet was rolled out, the corks of bottles of Washington State wine popped, speeches were made, contracts were signed, keys handed over, all in celebration of the formal delivery of Boeing's latest and greatest 747 to BA, which had ordered nineteen of them, plus a further twelve on option, in a deal worth a staggering $4.5 billion.

The airline's statisticians had worked out that, up to that moment, Boeing had supplied BA and its predecessor BOAC with a total of 170 airliners, going back to flying boats in 1941. Each one of these had been ferried from Seattle back to Britain without fuss or bother, and with little acclaim or ceremony. So casual onlookers might have been forgiven for wondering, Why the excitement over the 747–400? Apart from being BA's biggest-ever financial commitment to aircraft acquisition (and at the time the deal was signed, in late 1986, the largest in the history of the airline industry – although that was soon overtaken as the buying boom of the late 1980s accelerated), this was the aircraft which had been selected to take it into the twenty-first century on its prestigious and profitable long-haul routes. And the 747–400 was quite an airliner. Although the same fuselage size as its predecessor, the 300 series, it could fly 8470 statute miles non-stop, or 1300 miles further than the 300, it used up to 12% less fuel overall, and as much as 25% less compared with some of older 747s such as BA had in service. To help obtain this enhanced fuel consumption, the wings had been extended six feet, and each was tipped with a six-feet-high winglet, angled upwards and slightly outward.

Improved non-stop range was obtained through the designing into the horizontal tail of an additional tank to carry 3300 US gallons of fuel. This was an 'optional extra' offered by Boeing, but BA opted for it, even though it represented 1% of the basic cost of the aircraft. BA, in fact, ordered a total of 380 changes and options from the basic Boeing detail specification for the 400, costing in all some $6.8 million per aircraft. Among the major ones were tyre-pressure indication and door-mode indication, both displayed on EICAS (Engine Indicating and Crew Alert System) on the electronic flight-deck; automatic engine starting; provision for satellite communications; and crew rest areas – two of these were installed in each aircraft to offer brief periods of relaxation on the ultra-long flights for which the 400 was designed, one immediately behind the cockpit for the flight crew, and one upstairs in the tail, equipped with eight bunk beds, for the cabin crew.

Boeing obtained considerable weight reductions through extensive use of composite materials to replace traditional aerospace metals. Metal flooring in the cabin, for instance, was changed for panels made of graphite. But apart from the extended-range consideration, the two biggest changes for British Airways were the extension to the upper deck (first seen in the 747–300, which BA did not have in its fleet), and the replacement of the three-crew analogue cockpit with electro-mechanical instruments and a two-crew flight-deck with cathode-ray tube (CRT) displays. The majority of the information needed by the crew of two pilots flying the aircraft (the position of flight engineer was made redundant) was displayed on six 8″ × 8″ CRTs and could be called up at the touch of a button. In its total redesign of the cockpit, Boeing had reduced the number of flight-deck lights, gauges and switches from 971 to 365, and had, the company claimed, reduced the workload to one-half to one-third of earlier 747s.

BA ran in its new 747–400 on relatively short routes such as London to Philadelphia, Detroit, Pittsburgh and Montreal, to allow flight and cabin crews to obtain the 'feel' of the beast. It was then switched to the sort of ultra-long-haul routes for which it was destined at the outset – London to Australia and back, with only one stop (at Singapore) in each direction, London–Tokyo, London–Johannesburg. The important breakthrough on the Australia route was going to be Sydney–London where the 400 promised, against the prevailing winds, to carry a full load of 386 passengers and cargo without having to make an additional let-down in the Middle East for refuelling, thus saving two and a half hours' overall time for the journey.

On that sunny day in Seattle, it would have needed a very close observer of aviation to detect a sour note in the euphoric scene, but Boeing was three months late in delivering the aircraft to BA, which had thrown the airline's summer schedules considerably awry. The hold-up was due to the sheer immensity of the task which the manufacturer had taken on in developing a largely-new version of its long-serving 'jumbo jet', and in particular the grafting on of an electronic flight-deck, an extended wing, and a choice, requiring certification, of three different engine types – the Pratt and

Whitney PW4056, the General Electric CF6–80C2, and the Rolls-Royce RB211–524G, as selected by British Airways. At the same time, Boeing was also grappling with quality-control problems as it expanded its workforce to meet an unprecedented flood of orders for new airliners.

As with all of the other airlines which had ordered 747–400s, only to have them delivered late, BA was considering invoking penalty clauses in its contract with the manufacturer, and there had been some abrasive discussions between supplier and customer behind the scenes. But for public consumption on delivery day there was only sweetness in the air, with Lord King going out of his way to laud the US company and its product. The BA chairman assured his listeners:

> Such complaint as there may have been has been amicably and totally resolved. I should like to pay compliment to Boeing on the outstanding product that it builds, and without which today the world would not be able to go about its business.
>
> I am not aware that it is a crime to have built up such a successful business that you have a full order book. If this has led to some difficulties, I am confident that the situation that Boeing finds itself in is purely temporary. Yes, our 747–400s are a little later than originally promised, and there will be some discussion on this subject between us, but again let me assure you that any agreement reached will be amicable and satisfactory to all parties.

The order for the 747–400 was, in his opinion, probably the most important in the history of BA. The airline in 1988 carried 6.3 million passengers on its long-haul services and it was therefore essential, in order to remain competitive and to provide for growth in this important sector of the business, to have the best equipment on these routes through the 1990s and into the next century. Lord King said that apart from the orders and options for 747–400s, BA had orders and options at that time with Boeing for eighty-two other aircraft – 767s, 757s and 737s – worth about $5 billion.

> You will have deduced from this that British Airways is a very special customer for Boeing, and at the top of Boeing's list of favourite airlines. Against this background, we have, perversely, come under some criticism in the UK and Europe. It has been directed at the relationship between British Airways and Boeing. Some allege that we are a captive customer of Boeing.
>
> Our relationship with Boeing is nothing more or less than that between a competitive seller and a hard-nosed buyer. Our aircraft orders are based solely on commercial and technical criteria. Boeing, operating in the tough, free-enterprise environment of the USA, knows better than anybody that British Airways holds the option of buying what it wants, where it wants. It knows we have continuing dialogue with its competitors. It knows that we shop around for the best deal for British Airways, and will continue to do so. And Boeing knows that our commitment at the end of the day is to our bottom line, not theirs. Any order that Boeing wins from British Airways is on merit – and merit alone. We

expect Boeing to maintain and indeed improve its high standards relating to quality, price and delivery times.

Three years earlier, in London, 200 people – bankers and other financial types, lawyers, airline executives – sat down together at lunch to celebrate the completion of the deal which financed the British Airways 747–400s, a deal in which they had all been involved. Traditionally, airlines always bought their airliners, expecting to hang on to them for perhaps three-quarters of their working life before selling them, written down, to a small carrier in some distant land, or to a newcomer just breaking into the business. BA's financing of its 747–400 fleet was a total breakaway from this practice – an operating lease of a fairly pathfinding nature, highly compli-cated and involving five major banks, National Westminster, Barclays, Citicorp, Midland and Mitsubishi, plus a syndicate of some thirty-five others. Instead of the usual year and a half, the deal was pushed through in four months, since it was constructed during the run-up to privatisation and details of it had to be in the prospectus. At the end of it all the docu-mentation which it generated stood two feet high. What operating leases gave BA was the freedom to ride with the volatile airline market in the future. In general terms, the banks buy the aircraft from the manufacturers, and the airline leases them for short terms, say five, six or seven years, with the option of turning them back at those times if they no longer want them. This idea germinated in BA in 1983/4 when it financed some of the Boeing 737s in this way to replace its ageing Tridents. At that time the airline had no money of its own, the government would not allow it to borrow any more, and some way had to be found of 'hiring' the new aircraft. Fortune smiled, in that the manufacturers were desperate to shift airliners off their assembly lines, while the banking industry was beginning to become attracted to the idea of lending on the security of aircraft, having become disillusioned over lending in some other directions.

Tom O'Kane, BA Manager Finance Development, explained what the lease business was all about. There were, he said, two forms of lease – finance leases and operating leases. A finance lease was similar to a 100% mortgage on a house. The airline borrowed all the money, using the aircraft as security, and made regular repayments on the loan. The aircraft did not usually belong to the airline but the airline had the risks and rewards of ownership, including any increase or decrease in value. 'If you want to change it, you have to sell it and hope that you will get enough to cover the outstanding balance of the loan.'

An operating lease was defined as any lease which was not a finance lease. In an operating lease, the aircraft was owned by the lessor, who leased it to the operator – the lessee. The operator's liability only lasted until the first option date, at which point he could walk away with little or no penalty. O'Kane went on:

On the 747–400, we have option dates at years five and nine. The value of the aircraft at the option dates is underwritten by a combination of underwriting banks, manufacturers and British Airways, to be not less than a certain percentage of the aircraft purchase price. This is called an asset value guarantee, and gives the funding banks the security they need in the event that BA decides to return the aircraft and the aircraft value is not sufficient to cover the outstanding loan.

British Airways used operating leases to obtain a primary benefit of flexibility.

The purchase of aircraft generates capital allowances which can be used to reduce a company's tax liability. In many instances a lessor can make better use of these allowances than a lessee, and will be able to reflect that fact in the rentals charged to the lessee. This reduces the present value of the overall cost to less than it would have been if the aircraft had been purchased outright by the airline. Operating leases also provide off balance-sheet financing. This is not, however, the most significant factor in British Airways' decision to use operating leases. The primary benefits to BA that can be obtained from operating leases are, therefore, flexibility and cost. However, since BA is not the legal owner of the aircraft, it cannot do what it likes with it. We have a reasonable degree of flexibility, but we must also be aware of our obligations under the lease agreements, which can affect the aircraft's maintenance and operation.

The option dates at five and nine years mentioned by Tom O'Kane were important to British Airways against the cyclical nature of the air transport industry. Aircraft could be changed to take account of increasing, or perhaps decreasing, traffic, or the airline could take advantage of a technically more advanced type of aircraft which may have come on the scene. Airline services were being liberalised in many parts of the world, giving rise to changing patterns of services, and this was going to be the case particularly in Europe post-1992, when the opening of Common Market trade frontiers promised a rewriting of traditional networks.

The 747–400 prototype was rolled out of the Boeing factory at Everett, near Seattle, in late January 1988, a highly sophisticated version of the original 100 series aeroplane which emerged through those same doors twenty years earlier. Choosing it to replace its 747–100 fleet, which had been ordered by BOAC, and which at the time of the 400 series contract had an average age of 14.5 years, was a fairly straightforward decision for BA, in that there was really no competitor for the 747 in carrying power.

If only all such re-equipment decisions were as simple, the airline's senior executives sigh. Having selected the 747–400 airframe, the conundrum that followed was, which engine to power it? All three big Western-world engine manufacturers, General Electric, Pratt and Whitney, and Rolls-Royce, had products on offer that would do a pretty similar job. The contest developed into a two-horse race between GE and Rolls, the latter winning by a nose with its RB211–524D4D, generating 50 000 pounds of take-off thrust, largely on the basis of the financing package it was able to put together, low fuel consumption, advanced technology, and the fact that BA already had versions of the RB211 in its later B747–200s, B757s, and its TriStar fleet.

When BA started considering a successor to its long-range TriStars, having already selected the Boeing 767–300 to replace the short-range versions of that aircraft, things became exceptionally Byzantine. There were three contenders – the Boeing 777, the McDonnell Douglas MD 11, and the Airbus Industrie A340 – or maybe some more 747s. Each had a choice of engines on offer; each was accompanied by its financial package, and by swarms of eager salesmen who, in the nature of their breed, never gave up until the ink was dry on the contract. BA had grown the reputation of being a 'Boeing airline', but the MD 11, a three-engined airliner based on the airframe of the DC-10, but with a highly developed and sophisticated flight-deck and systems, was attractive – as was the A340. BA had never bought an airliner from Airbus, the European aerospace consortium formed by France, West Germany, Britain and Spain, but had had 'bequeathed' to it ten brand-new A320 150-seaters worth $340 million in the British Caledonian merger, so that it was able to assess the consortium's technology and its ability to keep its promises. Lord King lost no time after the BA–BCal marriage in going public that in BA's opinion the A320 was using about 9% more fuel for a given journey than was expected, due to a combination of an overweight airframe, greater drag, and a less efficient performance than promised for its twin CFM International (a consortium of General Electric and the French Snecma company) CFM56 engines. Airbus agreed that there was a shortfall, but disagreed with the 9% figure; they and the engine manufacturers had programmes to recover it.

There is no doubt that the BA management prized the new-found freedom given to them by the privatisation of the airline to select whatever airframe, engines and equipment they thought commercially viable. Previously the nationalised British carriers had had a lengthy history of government interference in their choice of equipment. 'Buy British' and 'support jobs in our factories' were cries which, although vote-winners, did not always produce the right sort of airliners for the state-owned airlines at the right time. Privatisation also gave BA the ability to act with speed in acquiring new equipment, rather than waiting for such decisions to queue for Cabinet approval.

So how does British Airways make these momentous choices on fleets of aircraft costing multi-billions, where a wrong decision, even with the escape chutes of operating leases, could send the company sliding into the red for years?

Many departments are involved, but particularly Planning, Purchasing, and Engineering. Is the aircraft on offer too big or too small? How many galleys and toilets can be built into it? Does it have sufficient emergency exits of the right kind? Is it compatible from the engineering and operating points of view with other airliners already in the fleet or on order (an important factor in BA's choice of both the Boeing 757 and 767, which have identical cockpits, enabling pilots to switch easily from one to the other)? Will it be fuel-efficient? What direct operating costs will it return? During this time, the airline's senior executives will be under intense pressure from the industry, the vendors of not only airframes and engines, but of seats, galleys, aviation electronics, and all the multifarious pieces of equipment which go to make up the modern airliner.

Being a large airline, British Airways is in a position to strike tough deals, and it is also able to point out that many of the smaller airlines around the world follow its lead in purchasing. It is also subject to continuing pressure to buy European (i.e. Airbus) rather than American (Boeing), thus supporting local rather than transatlantic industry (the wings of all Airbus airliners being designed and produced by British Aerospace). And going on in the background as BA examines the rival claims of the aircraft manufacturers in the United States and Europe is a long-running dispute between these two camps on subsidisation. The US Department of Trade alleges that Airbus Industrie is underpinned unfairly from a financial point of view by its four partner governments, both in the cost of research and development, design, and production, and in making sales abroad. The Europeans counter that the US aircraft-makers obtain hidden subsidies for their civil projects through the multibillion-dollar contracts which they obtain from the Department of Defense.

Airbus Industrie's view on this situation is that its American competitors have a share of some 85% of the total world aerospace market, so that without the presence of the Airbus consortium providing competition, freedom of trade under the General Agreement on Tariffs and Trade (GATT) would be non-existent. Airbus believes that the aircraft programmes which it has launched over the twenty years that it has been in existence will eventually produce profits, and that its sponsoring governments will receive a good return on the support which they have given – so satisfying the GATT rules. By 1989 Airbus was well established on the way towards achieving its stated aim of obtaining some 30% of the world market for airliners, with the A321 – a stretched version of its A320 – launched, with metal being cut for its A330/340 project, and with ambitious plans to double its production within five years. An important watershed was passed in the summer of 1988 when Airbus and Rolls-Royce signed a memorandum of understanding allowing the A330 to be offered to airlines with the RB211–524L engine at 65 000 lb of take-off thrust, for entry into service in summer 1994. It was the first time that a Rolls engine had been 'hung' on an Airbus product, and the feeling in the aerospace industry was that the agreement would widen the market considerably for the A330.

The Boeing 767–300 contracts which Lord King signed in London in February 1988 with Frank Shrontz, Boeing's Chairman and Chief Executive Officer, and Sir Ralph Robins, Rolls-Royce Managing Director, covered eleven aircraft, with options for a further fifteen, and were worth $2 billion. Deliveries were due to begin in November 1989. Of the $2 billion total, the Rolls-Royce share, for its RB211–524H engines, was $400 million. Lord King made the point that the Rolls engines, together with other British equipment on the 767, represented over 22% of the value of the total order – 'obviously good news for British industry and British jobs'. The 22% contribution did not include the ongoing value of future engine spares. BA's seating layout is 247 on domestic UK and European routes, and 267 on the Super Shuttle routes.

Over at Renton, Seattle, 4860 miles away from BA's headquarters at Heathrow, and at Everett thirty miles further north, the airline's decisions are turned into aircraft. Like all other Boeing Airplane Company's major customers, BA has offices and resident engineers in the Boeing works. The engineers constantly peer over the shoulders of their opposite numbers, making certain, in particular, that special modifications to the basic design specified in the contract are translated into metal. As one BA man said, referring to the 757, 'If you are paying something like $40 million for an aeroplane, you are entitled to make sure that you are getting what you want.'

It takes Boeing eight months to put a 757 together, from the moment when the first parts appear on the Renton assembly line to the moment when the new airliner rolls out through the factory doors to begin flight test. The wings and a major part of the fuselage for each aircraft of this type are made at Renton, but the rest of the sections come in from all over the US, and indeed the world. The nose is built in Wichita, the tail in Dallas, the engines in Derby, England. The aerospace industries of seventeen foreign countries, as far away as Japan and Australia, supply parts; the total number of suppliers reaches 4000, 200 of them from outside the US. There are 175 000 individual parts in each 757, and the constructors work to 75 000 separate technical drawings. There are 43 000 separate wires in each aircraft to be tied into bundles; each wing contains 30 000 rivets.

British Airways sends over its own pilots to test-fly, accept and deliver each new airliner from Boeing. They generally go on board after Boeing test pilots have completed around ten hours of test flying, carrying out several final-trials sorties which will include stall tests, touch-and-go landings, and go-rounds. The latter tries the advanced avionics fitted in the 757 which enable the pilots to fly the aircraft to within 14 feet of the ground, and then, at the flick of a switch, to climb away automatically into a holding pattern. A Boeing avionics engineer rides on board for these outings, spending most of his time in the bay in the belly of the aircraft containing the black boxes, and ready, if needed, to change faulty equipment in flight. A British CAA surveyor also accompanies these test flights to adjudge whether the new aircraft is fit to go on to the UK register. It is only after the pilots have expressed themselves totally satisfied with the product that the transfer of the aircraft from manufacturer to customer airline can be completed.

These handovers are usually low-key affairs in an office just off the Renton flight line. No money actually changes hands there – as another BA man said, 'Don't expect me to turn up with a briefcase full of gold bullion or dollar bills.' Watched by Federal Aviation Administration and CAA officials, Boeing and BA people shuffle papers to and fro across the table, signing here and there. Secretaries hurry in with cardboard boxes full of technical records, log books, and aircraft manuals. Keys – eight of them, mainly for the airliner's doors – are handed over, and at a significant moment one of the BA executives lifts a phone, dials the BA New York office on the other side of the US continent, and quietly gives the go-ahead for the transfer of funds into Boeing's account. Then it is all over, and somebody uncorks a bottle of cheapish sparkling wine for a toast to be drunk.

By the time the current order is filled by Boeing, British Airways will have thirty-four 757s in its mainline fleet, each powered by the Rolls-Royce RB211–535C engine, and two in its Caledonian Airways charter subsidiary with the E4 version of the same engine, giving 10% more fuel efficiency and a take-off thrust increase from 37 410 pounds to 40 000 pounds. Each one is flown virtually empty (the seats are put in at Heathrow) from Seattle overnight, a quarter of the way round the world, in around nine hours, generally arriving at BA's home base in the early morning with enough fuel still on board to fly on to Rome. As one of BA's 'ferry pilots' commented: 'Not bad for a medium-haul airliner.' Arrival of a new 757 creates no excitement at Heathrow. In Seattle they are a little more emotional. One hard-bitten Boeing worker commented, 'We're making two dozen airliners at any one time here at Renton, but when any one of them takes off for the first time, we all stand and watch, and it really gives you a good feeling inside.'

CHAPTER NINE

THE PILOTS: A FUN JOB
AND EASY TO DO?

When British Airways placed two advertisements for new-entrant trainee pilots, one in *The Daily Telegraph*, the other in the monthly aviation magazine, *Flight International*, it received 6800 replies. Those who made it as far as the interview stage were asked why they wanted to fly. The replies were invariably similar – always been interested in aeroplanes/they fly over my house, and I've watched them since I was a boy/my father was a pilot/ it's in the blood. When it came to having an idea of the career on which they were keen to embark, most were less certain. BA's interviewers found a *mélange* of theories about a pilot's life, a mixture which was summed up in a 'What I Want to Be when I Grow Up' essay by a schoolchild, published in BA's 757 Flight Crew Newsletter:

> I want to be a pilot when I grow up, because it is a fun job and easy to do. That is why there are so many pilots flying today. Pilots don't need much school, they just have to learn numbers so that they can read the instruments. I guess they should be able to read road maps so they won't get lost. Pilots should be brave so they won't get scared if it's foggy and they can't see, or if a wing or a motor falls off, they should stay calm so they'll know what to do.
>
> Pilots have got to have good eyes to see through clouds, and they can't be afraid of thunder and lightning because they are closer to them than we are. The salary pilots make is another thing I like. They make more money than they can spend. This is because most people think that plane flying is dangerous, except pilots don't, because they know how easy it is.
>
> There isn't much I don't like, except girls. Girls like pilots, and all the stewardesses want to marry pilots, so they always have to chase them away so they don't bother them. I hope I don't get airsick, because I get carsick, and if I got airsick I couldn't be a pilot – and then I'd have to go to work.

Misconceptions of this type are quickly dispelled when the tyros, both boys and girls, arrive at the Meadowbank Recruitment, Assessment and Selection Centre, a modest BA building just outside Heathrow airport, with the roaring Runway 27R at its rear and the equally noisy Bath Road in front. Inside is all academic quiet and calm, soothing but demanding. Here the sheep are sorted from the goats in a series of well-tried tests which leave little room for manoeuvre, for the aptitude to be a pilot is either there or it is not. Brain, hand, foot and eye co-ordination is vital if, in years to come, the young person facing up to selection is to fly an airliner safely down through the overcast into a foreign airport with a 30-knot crosswind blowing, at the end of a long, hard day. So one of the first tests which they tackle has been designed – by the RAF, and adapted by BA – to see whether such co-ordination is there. The applicant sits in front of a video screen, hand on a small control stick, feet on rudder pedals. In the middle of the screen is a cross; a white dot appears and zooms around the screen in random fashion. By moving the stick and the pedals, the applicant has to keep the dot in the centre of the cross. It looks simple but is infuriatingly difficult; strong-willed people have been reduced to speechless frustration in their attempts to do it. If the would-be pilot has co-ordination he will master the trick within the three tries which are allowed. If not, better forget the idea of flying and look for some other career.

Some of the young men and women who go to Meadowbank have done some private flying, either paid for from their earnings or with one of the university air squadrons. BA likes this, because it shows that they are both keen on aviating and of an enterprising nature, but to be accepted it is not necessary to have stepped into an aircraft as a pilot, or even as a passenger. There is a theory that there are advantages in taking young people who have not learned to fly, because they do not have to unlearn what they have been taught and relearn it all the BA way. Meadowbank is not the first step. Before being invited there, the candidates have to satisfy a number of other criteria – that they are British subjects, between 1.63 and 1.93 metres tall (flight-decks are becoming smaller since the days of what older pilots call 'gentlemen's aeroplanes', with the ability to get into the seats by walking round them rather than climbing over the central console), in what BA calls 'exceptionally good health', and with at least five GCSE passes, including English language, mathematics and a science subject, plus two further passes at A level, preferably maths and physics. The age limit is between eighteen and twenty-four, although BA will consider young people who are seventeen-plus and who intend to sit the relevant examinations at the end of the current academic year.

At Meadowbank they do other computer-based tests – designed, for instance, to indicate whether they have the ability to read instruments. All the tests are 'user-friendly'; no previous experience of handling the test devices is necessary. Written tests follow, all within one concentrated half-day. Those who succeed at this stage (and only 36% pass initial screening) are then invited back about a month later for further tests and assessment,

stretching, this time, over two days. Questionnaires evaluating their personalities and motivation are filled in, personal qualities probed using a series
of group exercises and interviews. At the end of it all a select few dozen are
told that they have been accepted for cadetships, subject to their supplying
satisfactory references. BA likes to get the selection right, not only because
it wants the right sort of pilot, but because mistakes are expensive, with the
cost of training over seventy weeks, to the stage of commercial pilot licence
and the ground stages of the air transport pilot licence, coming out at over
£50 000.

Captain Colin Barnes, British Airways Director of Flight Crew, said,
'Flying training is very costly, and there is, therefore, an obvious need to
predict success at the selection stage to avoid trainees dropping out of the
programme later on. The equipment which we have installed at Meadowbank provides us with an accurate and valid measure of a person's
potential as a pilot.' Dr Jack Wheale, the airline's Senior Occupational
Psychologist, added, 'Although only a limited number are able to meet the
extremely demanding standards, we do not want candidates to be
frightened into believing that only supermen and superwomen will succeed
in the tests, and none of the applicants should underrate their own ability.'
Even so, the whole selection procedure is naturally an extremely anxious
time for the young hopefuls, one of the great worries being whether they
will pass the stiff medical tests, tests which are given by both the airline and
by the CAA, which is the body responsible for pilot standards and for issu-
ing licences to fly.

The training takes place at the Flying Training College established by
British Aerospace alongside their manufacturing facility on the airfield at
Prestwick, on the Ayrshire coast in the west of Scotland. All of the training
costs are met by BA, as is full board at the College. This is done through a
loan, although the loan agreement involves no obligation to repay provided
that the student, after completing the course, accepts employment as a
pilot offered by BA, and provided that he or she remains in employment as a
pilot for at least five years. If, at the end of the course, the airline is unable to
make an employment offer as a pilot, the loan is written off.

Cadets spend seventy weeks in training at Prestwick, and it is no holiday
camp. From the first day they enter a community which is close-knit and
highly disciplined, and which has a strong 'flavour' of the airline which they
will be joining when they pass out (the Flying Training College takes cadets
from airlines other than BA; the first course from abroad, from the Hong
Kong-based Cathay Pacific, started in the spring of 1988). BA's cadets are
fitted with the airline's uniforms as they begin the course, and in their
flying training follow the airline's procedures and use its instruction
manuals. The course runs a five-day week, although some Saturday work is
also included; Sundays are free. Throughout the seventy weeks just two

holidays, totalling three weeks, are scheduled. The cadets are expected to live and work together in a residential atmosphere. Work is largely organised on a collective basis, but with plenty of private study.

The cadets live in a splendid old building close by the College. Adamton House is a former hotel which has been carefully refurbished as part of the overall £15 million project which established the College. It is equipped with 200 study-bedrooms, each with its *en suite* bathroom. Meals to a high standard are served in the house, with a choice from three main courses. New students spend their first two months in the classrooms without touching an aircraft, using the latest computer-based learning systems, with individual terminals operating from a central computer. Only after this do they make their first flight, with an instructor, in one of the College's fleet of eleven Swiss-made FFA AS 202 Wren single-engined aircraft. They then build up fifty hours' flying in the Wren, including aerobatics, after which they progress to the more advanced American-made Piper PA 28 Warrior II, of which the College has nineteen. A total of 105 hours are amassed in this type, the students learning instrument-flying and cross-country navigation. After that they move on to the College's most advanced aircraft, the American Piper PA 34 Seneca III; six of these twin-engined machines are in the fleet, and on them the cadets gain their instrument ratings in forty-five hours of flying. BAe bought all the aircraft brand-new when it set up the College.

Private pilot's licences are gained on the Wren. Interspersed with the flying, the cadets are in the classrooms grappling with a wide range of subjects, including meteorology, aerodynamics, electronics, radio aids, engines, the rules of the air, plus general and business studies. At every stage of the course they are studied and assessed. Failure to keep pace with the demanding and ever-intensifying curriculum, both on the ground and in the air, could result in a request to pack bags and leave. Towards the end of the course the cadets move on to flying in controlled airspace, and here the true worth of the Flying Training College being based at Prestwick airport, with its network of scheduled and charter airline routes, and with its busy traffic generated by the BAe factory, where the Jetstream 31 commuter airline is produced, becomes apparent. They learn what they will have to do when they join the line, fly along airways under air traffic control, into a modern airport pattern, joining the queue behind airliners ranging in size from Boeing 747s to Short 360s, then landing using the latest technical aids.

Back in the classrooms they build up 100 hours on the College's simulators to complement the total of 200 training hours in the air. The College has three types of simulators two Warrior II and three Seneca III for instrument-flying training, and two BAe 125–700 executive jets for what is known as LOFT training. LOFT stands for line orientated flying training, and under this system an airline flight between any two airports in the world can be exactly represented without the student ever leaving the classroom. The students are expected to fly at the times the airlines sometimes fly, late at night or in the early hours of the morning. Captain David Martin, first Principal of the College, whose own civil piloting experience began with BOAC in 1956 and concluded in 1985 as BA's Manager Flight Crew Training, said, 'We don't just fly at the College when the birds fly, between nine and five.' The College has done away with the old 'chalk-and-talk' teaching ethos. Its sophisticated learning machines include Carrel trainers on which cadets familiarise themselves with the systems, instruments and controls of the big jets which they will eventually fly.

Such an intensive course demands breaks for relaxation, and the College is also well equipped for that. It has its own library, recreation rooms and bar, dining-in nights, gymnasium and physical education instructor. Weekend trips are organised – venues can range from a nuclear-power station to a pop concert. And then, finally, comes the great day when the cadets have their commercial pilot's licences stamped and signed, and the wings badges which they have coveted over all those months of mental and physical stretching are issued. The new graduates also have an airline transport pilot's licence, 'frozen' because they will need to do a further 1000 hours' flying before it can be issued.

British Airways' first course at the BAe Flying College graduated in the spring of 1989, and the two women and fourteen men who had been its members had their pilot's wings presented to them by Lord King. The new pilots were posted to Lockheed TriStars, Boeing 737s and 757s, and Airbus A320s, and Lord King indicated that some of them would eventually move on to the airline's newest aircraft, the 747–400 and the 767–300. Captain Martin said of them, 'They have collectively and individually set standards which those who follow will find it hard to match.'

By the time that they graduated, a further 160 BA-sponsored cadets were in training at Prestwick, and by the end of 1989 the total had risen to 200. Gulf Air, a Middle East airline, had sent students, and British Aerospace was in negotiation with a number of other carriers. So critical had the world shortage of pilots become by then that BAe was advancing plans to establish a sister college in Australia, while the Prestwick college was being expanded to accommodate a total of 256 cadets.

Leaving Prestwick for BA's base at Heathrow airport, the new young pilots still have a lot of training to do. They join as junior co-pilots but go straight back to school for a further 4–5 months of learning. It is only then that they are allowed to take their place as first officers on line flights on a twin-engine jet such as the Boeing 737 or the twin turboprop BAe 748. But after that the sky is quite literally the limit, for later on, after gaining experience, skills and qualifications, they are able to apply for vacancies on the Boeing 757, Airbus A320, DC-10, Lockheed TriStar, Boeing 747 and Concorde fleets.

Whether they are the most junior first officer just joined, or the most experienced captain flying the latest 747–400 or supersonic Concorde, every BA pilot has to prove himself twice a year in a tough medical examination, and during recurrent training. The training takes place at the airline's training base at Cranebank, another complex on the edge of Heathrow airport, and involves doing checks and drills – in general, proving that they remain up to the airmanship standards required by BA and by the Civil Aviation Authority. The CAA, as the licensing authority, lays down standards for training, but BA has its own criteria, which are generally higher than the CAA's benchmarks. Recurrent training generally lasts about two days, during which what might be called routine emergencies, plus some others which very few pilots will ever experience in a lifetime career, are thrown at them. The beauty of the simulator is that the direst emergencies, such as two of four engines out on take-off, or an engine fire plus a loss of pressurisation during the descent, can be practised in totally realistic surroundings, but without endangering life or aircraft.

The simulator traces its lineage to the old Link trainer of World War 2. This looked like the truncated fuselage of a light aircraft anchored to the ground, and in it budding pilots sweated to co-ordinate rudder pedals and control column. Any connection between those early machines and today's multimillion-dollar high-tech devices is purely coincidental. The dozen or so BA simulators at Cranebank look from the outside like enormous boxes, standing on tall hydraulic legs which contract and expand as if in some sci-fi adventure. You enter the box across a sort of drawbridge and through a small door in the back, to be greeted inside by the flight-deck of an airliner, authentic in every detail right down to the indefinable aircraft smell. Through the cockpit windows there is a view of an airport, a view generated by a computer using thousands of tiny points of light. Such views used to be produced by remotely-controlled movie cameras ranging across a model board, but with the advance of computerisation these are now almost all gone – the last one in BA, which was at the BAe facility at Filton, Bristol, where Concorde pilots and flight engineers do their training, was replaced during 1988.

The instructor, who has his own control console at the back of each simulator, sets the training detail, which might be a 'flight' from Heathrow to one of the points on BA's route network, say Glasgow. The crew do their checks and start up, exactly as they would on an actual flight. The whine of the jet engines spooling up is heard. As taxying is initiated, bumps from the joins in the concrete can be felt in the cockpit, while the scene outside the windows changes until the runway, complete with lights and even the tyre marks typically made by aircraft landing, stretches away in front. The decision is made to go. Power is increased. The runway lights race past, faster and faster, until the control column is pulled back, and the sky fills the windscreen as the 'aircraft' climbs out. For the visitor to the simulator flight-deck, and for most crews doing their training, the atmosphere is so true to life by this stage that it comes as a shock when the instructor suddenly stops the action, leaving the picture outside the windows motionless like a freeze-frame on a video. The take-off can then be wound back, so that points with which the instructor may not be entirely happy can be discussed and tried again – and again, and again, if necessary. The flight is then resumed, passing through simulated mist, cloud, night, dusk and day if need be, with the instructor perhaps using his facility to build in turbulence of varying degrees, thunder, lightning, or even another aircraft on a near-collision course. On the approach into Glasgow, a representation of that airport, correct right down to the runway width and length and adjoining features, including traffic on nearby roads, even hotel neon signs, will come up. And just when the 'flight' is about to touch down, the instructor has the facility to make the image of an airliner pull on to the runway, so that the drills necessary for a go-round have to be brought into play.

At the end of it all, the pilots on the detail will probably feel much more wrung out than if they had been on a real flight-deck. The story is told – although it could just be a bit of salesmanship by the simulator manufacturers – of a new young pilot who was so taken up by his first simulator experience that, when told to abandon the aircraft in a mock emergency, he rushed through the access door and caused himself a considerable injury when he fell down the steps on to the concrete floor of the simulator hall.

For British Airways simulator training is a considerable money-saver, for although its simulator complex has had some £60 million invested in its buildings and equipment over the years, with the latest 747–400 facility costing £9.5 million of that total, to do the work on real aircraft would cost between ten and thirty times as much, depending on aircraft type, as carrying it out on the ground. Such figures not only include the costs, in fuel, engineering and so on, of operating such aircraft on training schedules, but also take into account the fact that they would be away from revenue-earning service – which would mean that additional airliners would have to be bought for the fleet. The airline also makes anything up to £3 million each year from leasing simulator time out to other airlines – ranging from the big US carriers to CAAC, the national airline of China. BA also offers a wide range of other flight operations tuition at its flight-crew training centre, which is equipped with the latest computerised teaching aids. As at the Flying Training College 'chalk-and-talk' training is a thing of the past.

A further major advantage of the simulator is that it can be kept 'in the air' for far longer each day than any airliner. The only day when Cranebank falls silent is Christmas Day. For the rest of the year these sophisticated devices operate up to twenty hours a day, and it is by no means unusual for a training detail to begin late at night and to continue through the small hours of the morning. The simulators have now become so sophisticated, in fact, that both the American FAA and the British CAA have agreed their use in conversion training – that is when pilots change from one airliner type to another – under the principle of what is known as 'zero flight time'.

Under zero flight time, pilots are able to switch – so long as the two types of aircraft involved are fairly similar to each other – without actually having flown the new type in the air. Well over 10 000 pilots have converted in this way in the United States, and BA gained permission from the CAA in 1987 to introduce the system on one of its two 737 simulators and on its 757. It also uses its simulators for new training and recurrent training in automatic landing. But although they never leave the ground at Cranebank, there are no soft options for pilots and flight engineers in the various types of simulator training there, and as the never-ending process to maintain safety standards goes on, members of air crew who do not satisfy the instructors are asked to go back and repeat the checks until they get them right.

The task of preventing accidents and incidents, in addition to investigating them after they have happened, is that of the Director of Safety Services. Safety Services keeps in close touch with the airline's engineering, flight-crew and cabin-crew departments as the monitor of safety standards, and when details of an incident to another airline, anywhere in the world, come in, the question of whether it could happen to BA is immediately posed. Little incidents which might not be important in themselves could just turn into a trend. Such trends are publicised throughout the airline by means of a monthly air safety review listing all incidents, from sticking cabin doors to major emergencies. An open exchange is considered vital, and everybody involved is encouraged to report things which have gone wrong. Pilots are also able to report anonymously, through a scheme called CHIRP, run by the Institute of Aviation Medicine at the Royal Aerospace Establishment in Farnborough.

While very much a part of BA, Safety Services is also a department apart, with the right of access to any source of information, and with no doors closed to it. In practice, however, it is most unusual for the big whip to be cracked. The search for safety is a matter which unites one and all in aviation. Everybody is usually anxious to help. The Director of Safety Services reports directly to the Chief Executive, and his branch is independent of all other departments within the airline. There is a Board Air Safety Review Committee, meeting once a month to review all incidents which have occurred to BA airliners, and discussing preventive measures. It is chaired by a main board director and its membership consists of virtually the entire BA board.

Further tasks of Safety Services include security, with members of the team regularly checking buildings and property belonging to the airline all over the world, and safety on the ground – covering the aircraft ramp, hangars and workshops, offices, and terminal buildings. The remit also embraces passengers, both on the ground and in the air. Trying to ensure that the airline's paying customers take notice of the safety briefings before flights, bring only a modicum of hand baggage on board instead of, as appears at some airports, their entire personal possessions, and then stow that baggage tidily in overhead bins or under the seats, is a never-ending endeavour. Badly-stowed luggage could, at worst, fatally impede evacuation if there was a real emergency, or at least cause injury. BA has had several cases where airliners have had to turn back to the terminal while taxying out to the runway because an overhead locker has burst open through the sheer volume of goods stuffed into it, and passengers have been struck on the head by falling objects, usually bottles of duty-free.

BA's forecasts indicate that it will have to recruit between 150 and 200 pilots a year between now and the end of the century to keep pace with the projected expansion of the business, and to replace those of its pilot force, now numbering 2400 with the arrival of some 500 from British Caledonian, who have to retire compulsorily at fifty-five. For about ten years up to 1987, the airline did little pilot recruiting; it had more than enough experienced men available because it was changing over from three-crew to two-crew airliners, pilot productivity was rising, and for part of that time the industry was in recession. As a result, the average age of the pilot force rose and by the end of 1987 the youngest BA pilot was turned thirty; by the year 2007 all would be drawing their pensions. It was this realisation which hastened the recruitment of new entrants through Prestwick, and led to a stepping-up of employment of experienced pilots through direct entry. These, generally in their late twenties or early thirties, come from other airlines, from general aviation, from the Services, and from helicopter companies (these last must have fixed-wing flying experience as well).

The airline has also been recruiting flight engineers to its force of over 500, for although they are often thought to be a 'dying breed' with the advent of the two-man cockpit, BA has extensive fleets of three-man-cockpit airliners – the 200 series, 747s, TriStars, DC-10s and Concordes – and will continue to have them well into the 1990s, and in some cases beyond the year 2000. After that, the flight engineer will go the same way as the radio officer, the navigator, and the days when the flight-deck complement of airlines numbered as many as five.

The bunching in the ages of BA pilots has meant that, although first officers can expect promotion to senior first officer after six years, the step up to captain has been taking co-pilots up to nineteen years from the moment of joining – a date which rules the progression of every pilot throughout his career with the airline. This lengthy wait for a command, involving some

800 men, has been the subject of considerable dissatisfaction. The forecast is that the situation will improve as the business expands, and as an increasing number of captains move into retirement, so that by 1996 BA captaincies should be attainable ten years after first putting on the uniform.

Dissatisfaction also resulted from the merging of the BA and British Caledonian pilot forces, following the takeover, with up to seventy-five BCal captains facing demotion. Some of these, in their forties, will most likely not regain their commands and will therefore retire as co-pilots, while young first officers, of whom BCal had a fair proportion, must expect to wait far longer for a command than was the case in their old company.

One area where seniority plays no part is in the selection of the nucleus of forty-five management pilots and ten management flight engineers who, although continuing to fly the line, have additional responsibilities, such as being in charge of the flight crews of the various fleets of different airliners, laying down technical standards, and training. They are all selected on merit, but before appointment have to go through the airline's flight management assessment centre where, among other attributes, their ability to get on with people, management skills, and understanding of the needs of the airline, are probed.

BA's flight crew are able to 'bid' on a seniority basis for the types of aircraft and routes they will fly, and here opinions differ enormously between the merits of long-haul, where crews can be away from base and home for as long as fourteen days, and short/medium-haul, where tours of duty do not generally last longer than two or three days at the most. The pill of long sectors on long-haul is sweetened by special allowances, but so is what is generally considered by BA pilots to be the least attractive job in the airline – back-up shuttle crew, entailing much waiting around in the crew room, and never really being sure where or when you are going to fly and where you might spend the night. There is not so much laying over of crews in exotic spots thousands of miles away as there was before BA was pulled round, and coping with time-zone changes is hard on the human frame. But in the end it comes down to a matter of personal preference, and occasionally a long-haul pilot changes to the 'bus services' around Europe as a way of obtaining his command, and finds the life not too terrible after all. One airliner which most pilots would like to lay their hands on is the Concorde, and a few obtain the chance. BA accepts switches between fleets, but it does apply freeze periods to each aircraft type – five years in the case of the 747 and TriStar, three years for the rest – because of the cost of conversion training, and loss of productivity while that training is being carried out.

The retirement age of fifty-five is fixed by BA and is a contentious topic in crew rooms and wherever else pilots meet. The CAA rules that UK-registered airline pilots can fly on to sixty, always providing they keep passing the medicals. Many BA men see no reason why this criterion should not be applied to their airline since at fifty-five most of them are at the peak of their experience and skills, with hundreds of thousands of pounds of training and retraining behind them – all of which is wasted when the day for the gold watch comes along. The traditional BA view was that to keep its pilots on to sixty would make the careers of the younger, thrusting generations even more frustrating, while a secondary view is that, after fifty-five, some pilots at least are not quite as alert and dynamic as they believe they are, particularly when it comes to operating in airways and at airports which are becoming more and more crowded. However, during 1989 the airline had a significant change of heart, and began offering short-term contracts to pilots and flight engineers who had reached the normal fifty-five retiring age.

The matter came up when a senior first officer with the 747 fleet wrote to the airline:

> When we are taking a very close look at our cost levels with regard to our competitors, it is significant that two out of the top three most profitable airlines in the world, namely Virgin and Singapore Airlines, have a large proportion of pilots – principally captains – previously employed by British Airways who were forced to leave reluctantly when they reached fifty-five.
>
> Not only are these airlines able to pay below-average salaries – because of the availability of these pilots with their existing pensions – but they are also able to save very considerable sums in training costs, and to have opportunities for expansion that might otherwise be limited by a shortage of qualified aircrew. It might seem expedient internally to retire higher-paid pilots when the job can be done more cheaply by those who are younger. The wider ramifications of this, applied across the economics of the airline industry, are difficult to quantify, but are likely to counteract any such savings many times over.

Phil Stubbs, Human Resources Manager, Flight Crew, replied:

> We constantly review employment policies with regard to flight crew, and we have decided to retain fifty-five as the compulsory retirement age. However, we now have the facility to offer fixed-term contracts to those pilots and flight engineers who have reached their compulsory retirement age. In the case of captains, this is to continue as co-pilots only. The contract will be for a fixed term of one year, but further fixed-term contracts may be offered, depending on our requirements.
>
> With regard to those ex-British Airways pilots employed by other airlines, many left British Airways under early retirement severance schemes in the days when we had a surplus of flight crew. Many now want to return.

At retirement age in BA a captain can expect to be earning a pensionable salary of some £50 000, plus allowances. A cadet from Prestwick will start at around £16 000 on being offered his or her contract. Direct-entry pilots from other airlines generally come in in the region of £20 000. With certain small exceptions, all pilots of equivalent rank earn the same whatever airliner type they are flying – that is, the captain of a Boeing 737 will be on the same scale as the captain of a Concorde. Pay scales and conditions of service are negotiated by the airline's management with the pilots' union, BALPA, of which all but the smallest handful are members.

After long years of heart-searching, during which the view was heard from some managements and some pilots that the only place on board an airliner for a woman was on the other side of the cockpit door, BA opened its flight-decks to women in 1987, and the first, Lynn Barton, came aboard in April that year. She was followed closely by two others, Wendy Barnes and Jill Devlin. All three were experienced pilots with other airlines. After intensive conversion training, they began flying as co-pilots with BA in the autumn of 1987, Lynn on 747s, Wendy on 1-11s, and Jill on the BAe 748. Lynn Barton had a double distinction, for not only was she Britain's first woman pilot to be licensed to fly a 'jumbo', but she had also been sponsored by BA at its own training college at Hamble near Southampton ten years earlier – shortly before the airline stopped all pilot recruitment. By summer 1988, the number of women pilots flying for BA had increased to fourteen, while the first intake of cadets at Prestwick included two. BA's pilot management expressed itself keen to obtain more girl cadet recruits (there is no male/female quota in the airline), but was disappointed by the small numbers which initially came forward.

Although nostalgia is always in vogue among pilots (the story of the BEA man who, in the early post-war days of flying in Scotland, would don dark glasses and tap his way up the aisle between the passengers to the cockpit with a white stick, declaiming, 'If nobody else will fly this thing, I will', still goes the rounds), the business today is very futuristic. Automatic aids on the flight-deck are turning the flier into a systems manager. Will there be sufficient job satisfaction to attract young men and women into careers with the airline in the twenty-first century? Captain Barnes:

> The speed of technological change is exciting to pilots, and the amount of information which is now displayed has made the modern aeroplane easier to fly than its predecessors. But the environment in which we fly is becoming increasingly demanding. The nature of the job may have changed, but you can never be bored. There is too much to do.
>
> The pilot may not be handling the controls, but he will be programming the automatics – on which it would be easy to become too dependent. We emphasise the necessity to hand-fly the aeroplane, and pilots like to do this anyway. Some pilots believe there has been an erosion of the captain's status and authority. In the days of Imperial Airways the captain was the company's representative in every sense. Since then many other departments in the airline have become involved in mounting operations. Despite this, everybody still looks to the captain for command decisions, and I believe that the status and standing of the airline pilot remains high.

CHAPTER TEN

BA 504 READY FOR TAKE-OFF

British Airways Flight 504, a Boeing 757–200, named on the nose Caernarfon Castle but known to the airline as Kilo Delta, wheels slowly on to the threshold of Heathrow airport's 3900-metre runway 27 Right. Three Lockheed TriStars, two in the colours of BA, the third from Air Canada, have just thundered down the same runway at brief intervals one after the other, while Kilo Delta waited at the holding point. Now a British Airways BAC1–11 airliner is just lifting off and it is the turn of the 757.

Senior First Officer Phil Bright, sitting in the right-hand seat on the flight-deck, talks to air traffic control (ATC): '504 now entering runway 27 Right', and receives a crisp acknowledgement. The 1–11 is rapidly becoming a speck against the sky in the distance, and ATC is on the radio: '504 is clear to take-off.'

Captain Clive Elton, in the left-hand seat, is making the take-off. Phil Bright calls out the speed as Kilo Delta accelerates. '80 knots.' And then: 'Rotate.' The control column is eased back and the flat landscape of Heathrow airport, as seen through the cockpit windows, is suddenly replaced by cloud. The accelerating rumble of the aircraft's ten tyres on the runway pavement ceases, the two Rolls-Royce RB211–535C jet engines exude a roar of controlled power, and Kilo Delta, all 85.8 tonnes of her, soars effortlessly into the air to fly the afternoon scheduled service to Rome, Fiumicino.

The moment is the culmination of a lengthy period of preparation in which hundreds of people in the airline have played a part: people from flight planning and operations control, from engineering and catering, from marketing and ground operations, and from many other departments. For Captain Elton, thirty years with the airline and now a senior training captain (and before BA a Canberra bomber pilot with the RAF), the flight began two hours earlier when he left home to drive the twenty miles to the airport – the segment of the journey which most pilots will tell you they consider the most dangerous.

Check-in at the crew reporting desk at Heathrow is an hour before scheduled departure time, and it is then that they learn who is to be the partner on the flight-deck, details of the aircraft which has been allocated to the service, and the stand on which it is parked – in this case Charlie 24, 'a good one', says Clive Elton, as it is reasonably near the take-off point of runway 27 Right and so does not involve too much manoeuvring and taxying.

Behind the girls handing out this information sits the crew controller who, with the task of ensuring that some 200 BA flights each day have pilots with sufficient duty hours, has to be something of a cross between a juggler and a psychologist. The psychology bit comes in when a crew returns from flying a service and still has enough legal hours to take on another for which BA, for various reasons, might have suddenly found itself short of a crew. Under the bidline system there is no compulsion on such occasions, but a smile and a kind word sometimes work wonders. 'It helps to know the people you work with,' the crew controller grins.

British Airways keeps stand-by crews around the crew reporting centre against the eventuality of pilots or co-pilots not turning up for flights for whatever reason – accident, or illness perhaps – and has other crews on stand-by at home. In the case of an airliner going sick, ops control gets into the juggling business, bringing up a spare, perhaps of another type, and in the direst cases transferring passengers to a competitor. Crew control and ops control work round the clock, 365 days a year. 'Like the Windmill Theatre,' says one of the staff there, 'we never close.'

Check-in complete, Clive Elton does a quick scan of the multifarious notices on the boards, ranging from 'must read' to bills advertising theatrical shows, then moves on to the area where flight briefing takes place. It is there that he meets his co-pilot for the day. Phil Bright has been with British Airways for eighteen years, having entered as a cadet from the old College of Air Training at Hamble. He is just being promoted to a training co-pilot, and hopes for his command in a few years' time. Although the two have flown together before, there are no permanently fixed flight-deck crews in BA, the airline taking the view that as everybody is trained to the same standard they can be freely intermingled on a fleet-by-fleet basis. The BA 757 fleet has around 350 pilots, and will expand considerably when the airline begins to receive its new Boeing 767s. The two aircraft types have similar flight-decks, and the cockpit crews will be cleared to fly both.

Flight briefing in BA is on the principle of 'do it yourself', with massive back-up from computers. FICO comes first, Flight Information and Control of Operations. Clive Elton punches the 504 flight number into a keyboard, is told by a message on a video screen to wait a moment, and a few seconds later the printer starts to pour out information on winds and weather; on every airport along or near the route to Rome to which the aircraft might conceivably have to divert – from Heathrow to Manchester, from Paris to Brussels, from Geneva to Turin, from Nice to Naples; on navigation hazards (Mount Etna is active in Sicily); and on snags to Kilo Delta, which has, it is learned, a minor problem with the air supply from its auxiliary power unit (there is a small doubt whether the APU will generate sufficient air for engine starting – in which case, a ground air-supply unit will be called up). As the printer continues to chatter, the captain comments, 'Looks as if it will run from here to Rome.' When it finishes the briefing paper in fact stretches to nine feet.

A second computer with an acronym, this time SWORD, is less expansive. Its brief runs to four feet of paper only, but this carries vital information on the fuel state of Kilo Delta, and of the waypoints over which the aircraft will pass on its route between Heathrow and Fiumicino. What does SWORD stand for? A passing wag suggests 'Sure way of running dry', but the real answer is System of Worldwide Operational Route Data.

The pace of preparation is now hotting up. The captain and co-pilot move to the weather briefing, which will obviously have an important bearing on the amount of fuel they take with them. There is a generally unstable look about the weather over Europe, with a nasty-looking little low-pressure area over Sardinia which could give some turbulence on the approach into Rome and, unusually, a strongish headwind from the south. SWORD has calculated that for this particular flight Kilo Delta will need 7629 kilos of fuel for the 2 hour 9 minute trip, an extra 881 kilos for contingencies (giving another 15 minutes' flying time), an extra 1347 kilos for possible diversions (17 minutes), an extra 1703 kilos in reserve (30 minutes), and an extra 300 kilos for taxying out to the runway at Heathrow – making 11 860 kilos, or 11.8 metric tonnes, of fuel in all. KD could carry up to 35 tonnes. Fuel is the captain's decision, and it is decided to add enough for an additional ten minutes' flight time, in view of the reported weather conditions. There is a cost-conscious reminder on the SWORD briefing that each 1000 kilos uplifted costs the airline £15 in extra weight carried, and general wear and tear, but nobody would ever be rebuked for erring on the side of caution.

By the time Clive Elton and Phil Bright decant from the crew bus at stand Charlie 24, the request for extra fuel has been passed on to the fuel company, and the Jet A1, the type of kerosene used by most airlines today, is being pumped into the tanks. On this occasion the captain does the walk-round inspection of the outside of the aircraft (the co-pilot will do it at Rome before the return journey), paying particular attention to the wheels, brakes and tyres, the engines, and the moving surfaces on wings and tail, and the surprising number of communications aerials.

The cabin crew of six, led by Cabin Services Director (CSD) John Hancock, is already on board, and there is, despite the fact that British Airways is a big airline, a relaxed, almost 'family' atmosphere as aircrew, cabin crew, the ground engineer and the flight despatcher meet and greet.

The cockpit is not over-large. Captain and co-pilot settle in, hanging their uniform jackets in a small wardrobe space at the rear, adjusting their seats up and down, forward and back. Clive Elton is not pleased to be told that one of the four lavatories on board is not working – 'definitely not good with a fairly full load of passengers'. The ground engineer pokes his head through the cabin door, proffering the aircraft technical log for the captain to sign. One copy goes into the airline's records, another is left at whatever station the aircraft is leaving from – just in case anything goes wrong. 'She's all yours,' says the engineer, ducking out of the cockpit.

He is immediately replaced by the flight despatcher, with his distinctive red cap, whose job has been to make sure that the 1001 items which go into a flight have all come together for an on-time departure. The Red Cap reports and also disappears. Meanwhile the passengers are boarding, 139 in all, one in a wheelchair, plus two babies – thirty-two in club class, 107 in the economy section at the rear. As each one steps off the jetway he or she is greeted by John Hancock and a stewardess and directed to the correct seat according to the number on their boarding card.

Kilo Delta has a precise take-off slot in Heathrow's crowded flying pro-gramme. It means that the aircraft must be at the end of the runway at two minutes before the hour and Captain Elton is now anxious to start. The control column is eased back and forth; the litany of checks between pilot and co-pilot begins.

'Exterior inspection?' 'Completed.'

'Cockpit preparations?' 'Completed.'

'Passenger signs?' 'Auto.'

'Flight instruments?' 'Set.'

'Park brakes?' 'Set.'

The two men then go through a briefing on the procedure for take-off, plus actions to be taken if there is an emergency. 'It looks as if there might be a bit of turbulence on the climb, so we'll keep the seat-belt signs on for a while,' says the captain. He then has his first word over the PA with the passengers, now settled in their seats, giving them the weather conditions *en route* and some of the waypoints – 'crossing the French coast between Dieppe and Le Havre, and approaching Rome over Genoa and Pisa'.

The Red Cap makes a final appearance on the flight-deck with the load sheet. He assures that word of the disabled passenger will be signalled ahead to Rome so that the lady can be transferred to a clever wheelchair there which can be pushed up and down steps. The Red Cap says his goodbye, the passenger jetty is driven away. On a word from the CSD, the cabin staff lock and arm the doors.

'Speedbird 504, permission to start for Rome?'

'504, stand by for start.'

A brief pause. Then '504. Clear to start.'

Because of the slight worry over the APU, the decision has been made to start the right engine on the stand. A switch in the overhead roof panel is turned, and the RB211 runs up perfectly. The engineer is now on the apron, his headphones and mike plugged into an external socket on Kilo Delta, talking to the flight-deck. In a phrase that is straight out of Biggles, he is requested: 'Chocks away, please.'

Permission is sought and gained to push back. The eight brakes on KD are released, and the aircraft comes alive as the powerful tractor that has linked up to her nosewheel leg takes the strain. The CSD puts his head round the flight-deck door to report: 'All doors are to automatic.' This means that the automatic escape slides will deploy if the doors are opened.

As the aircraft moves slowly backwards, the cabin staff are giving the safety briefing – in English, then repeated in Italian. 'We shall be flying at a height of 37 000 feet . . . Hand baggage must not obstruct the aisles or emergency exits . . . In your seat pockets you will find a flight safety card . . . The emergency exits are being pointed out to you now.'

The left engine is started during the push back. Kilo Delta comes to a halt for the tractor to be disengaged. The engineer has disconnected his link with the aircraft and waves to indicate all is well. Captain Elton acknow-ledges with a thumbs-up. He reports, 'Clear left.' Phil Bright reports, 'Clear right.' The throttles are inched forward. Kilo Delta is on her way.

On the way to the runway, KD passes ranks of other BA airliners, mainly other 757s and their smaller brothers, the Boeing 737, lined up noses in to the terminal building, setting down or picking up passengers and freight. An Air France A300 Airbus alights on the runway ahead in a roar of reverse thrust. John Hancock reports, 'All secure aft.'

'Any complaints?' enquires the captain.

'Not so far,' says the CSD, going to strap himself in for take-off.

Kilo Delta is airborne a few minutes late due to air traffic control delays. As the big airliner thrusts up towards the overcast, its altimeters winding on at the rate of 3000 feet a minute, there is intense concentration in the cockpit, but the niceties are still observed.

'Gear up, please,' requests the captain. The co-pilot shifts the big lever in front of him. There is a rumble and a clunk as the wheels fold away. Then, at the request of the captain, the flaps are moved in progressively. Kilo Delta approaches 6000 feet, and a further series of checks begin.

'Landing gear?' 'Up and off.'

'Flaps?' 'Up.'

'Altimeters?' 'Set and cross-checked.'

Kilo Delta arrives over the Midhurst beacon as planned at 6000 feet, bumping gently through thick cloud, then suddenly bursting through into brilliant blue. It is the moment that every pilot appreciates. 'Isn't that nice?' says Clive Elton. He has been flying the aircraft up to this point, but now engages the autopilot. The high-workload period of take-off and climb-out is over, and there is a feeling of pressure being relaxed slightly. But it is far from plain sailing from now on. The crew has requested a cruise height of 37 000 feet, but the controller on the ground below can only offer 27 000 feet. Phil Bright is now the handling pilot and Clive Elton is looking after the communications. He tries the controller again.

'Speedboard 504, looking for something higher than 27 000 feet.'

'504, all the levels around you are filled up. There are five more aircraft in a bunch.'

Captain and co-pilot scan the skies outside the cockpit windows. There are no other airliners to be seen. 'A good justification for taking on the extra fuel,' Clive Elton muses.

At the lower level, where the air is thicker and warmer, the RB211s will use more fuel than in the higher, colder, thinner air. One of the on-board computers is already telling the crew that at the requested flight level KD will land at Rome at six minutes past five with 4.8 tonnes of fuel left in the tanks, but that if the flight goes the whole distance at 27 000 feet this will be reduced to 3.8 tonnes. It will cost a tonne of fuel to stay down.

'I don't know how we would manage without these marvellous devices,' Clive Elton says. 'It would take humans hours to work out these figures.'

'Yes,' agrees Phil Bright, 'and computers never get a headache.'

By this time the rate of climb has been slowed to 2000 feet per minute, the thrust-management computer adjusting the power to give the most economical fuel burn. Each 211–535C engine is able to generate 37 400 lbs of thrust at take-off – more than all three engines on the Tridents which the 757 superseded in BA's fleet – but they are seldom operated at full bore. For the departure on auto-throttle out of Heathrow, the thrust was de-rated 12% and there was plenty of power to spare, so saving both fuel and wear on the power-plant.

Kilo Delta's progress across the English Channel and into northern France is shown graphically on the seven-colour cathode-ray tubes which are a feature of the 757's high-tech – 'all singing, all dancing' is the favourite description in the aviation industry – cockpit. In front of each pilot is the appropriate segment of the compass rose (in Americanese the horizontal situation indicator), computer-generated, and free from flicker even when the aircraft may be bouncing about the sky. On one display KD appears as a small triangular symbol superimposed on a map of France, moving slowly down the screen as the flight proceeds

The aircraft's future track across the map is shown as a magenta line from waypoint to waypoint, waypoints being radio beacons on the ground below, each identified on the screens in the cockpit by (in Europe) three-letter codes. The time of arrival at each waypoint can be put up on the screen by the crew and displayed next to the appropriate waypoint. Other options for the pilots include superimposing airports close to the route, superimposing other navigation beacons in the vicinity, and laying the weather radar over the map. It is also possible, at the touch of a switch, to change the scale of the moving map so that the distance represented between the top and bottom of the screen can be 10, 20, 40, 80, 160 or 320 miles.

On the screen above the compass in this remarkable EFIS (Electronic Flight Instrument) system is what pilots used to know as the artificial horizon, now called the attitude director indicator. Two screens in the centre of the instrument panel monitor the three stages of each engine, giving constant read-outs of fuel consumption, temperature, vibration levels, and other parameters. This is the EICAS (Engine Indicating And Crew Alert System), and it is on the upper of the two screens that warning messages appear if anything is going wrong with any of the aircraft's systems, all of which are constantly monitored electronically throughout the flight. There is an astonishing amount of computer wizardry in an airliner like the 757, and it is this untiring back-up for the pilots which made the two-crew airliner feasible, signalling the retirement of the flight engineer from this type of aircraft. The EFIS screens in front of both captain and co-pilot are independent of each other, so that one pilot can call up different information to that being displayed on the screen of his colleague. There is a large element of back-up in the systems, so that in the extremely rare event of a failure alternatives can be selected. There are still some electro-mechanical dials on the 757 flight-deck and beside the video displays they look very old-fashioned.

On the ground before the flight began, Phil Bright programmed in the latitude and longitude of the spot where Kilo Delta was parked (not just Heathrow airport, but stand Charlie 24 – it is that accurate) and the route, already held in the BA data base, to be followed from Heathrow to Rome. Now airborne the aircraft will turn itself on to new tracks on reaching the waypoints, the crew having activated the lateral navigation system shortly after take-off.

Nearing Paris, Kilo Delta is still ploughing along at 27 000 feet. Clive Elton says he will 'drop a hint', and presses the transmit button. 'Any chance of a higher level?'

A French air traffic controller comes back immediately. 'Negative, sir.'

'Well, that was brief and to the point,' says the captain to his co-pilot.

In cloud near the French capital, the engine anti-icing system is switched on and the captain addresses the passengers over the PA, apologising for the lower altitude – 'apparently it is a busy day up here'. He holds out hope that the higher level might be attainable by the Swiss border, but he has hardly finished speaking when French ATC is back.

'Speedbird 504, climb to flight level 37 zero.'

The new altitude is dialled in, and Kilo Delta moves up out of the murk into blue sky once again. Still no other aircraft are to be seen, but the radio waves are full of accents from all over the world – British, American, Swiss, Italian.

Back in the cabin, the stewards and stewardesses are serving a light meal to Club Europe passengers. There is a starter of kiwi fruit, orange segments and banana in passion fruit syrup, followed by hot snacks comprising fried chicken fillet, beef brochette, asparagus spears rolled in bacon, and liver paté puff garnished with a savoury mushroom and cherry tomato. Then comes a cheese course – Stilton and Red Leicester, with crackers and butter. To drink, there are coffee or tea, wines from Bordeaux, Burgundy, Champagne and the Rhine, spirit and liqueur miniatures, and beers, minerals and cordials. For the Club passengers the drinks are free; for those in economy, who receive a boxed meal, there is a pay bar, although the mixer drinks are not charged.

The CSD brings crew meals to the flight deck – two different dishes, one beef, one pork, because, for obvious reasons, the two pilots are not allowed to eat the same type of food. Who has which is the captain's prerogative, but Clive Elton takes a democratic line and offers Phil Bright first choice. The aircraft has steadied on 37 000 feet in bright sunshine. The captain goes on the PA to point out the Alps, glistening with snow, through a gap in the cloud-bank. Geneva is down to the left. British Airways encourages its pilots to adopt a relaxed and friendly approach on the public address system. Flying the shuttle routes in the summer, Clive Elton listens in to BBC Radio 3 and then relays the cricket scores to the passengers. However, different approaches are needed for different flights. The businessmen and women on the shuttle have heard it all before, but the once-a-year customers on holiday routes are reassured by a chatty commentary.

Now the captain tells Kilo Delta's passengers, just finishing their meals, 'We will be arriving at Rome in an hour from now. Weather conditions continue to be cloudy along our route. The weather in Rome is humid, with a fresh breeze.' And he adds, 'You should put your watches forward to 1812 – like the overture.'

John Hancock takes over the PA. 'The cabin staff will be coming through the cabin with duty-free goods shortly. A list of goods and prices will be found in the back of *High Life*.' *High Life* is British Airways' monthly in-flight magazine.

Milan Volmet weather service is giving out a recorded report for various airports in Italy, the accent of the Englishman who made the recording in contrast to the vowel sounds of the Italian air traffic controllers who are now filling the airwaves with their English. The captain tries his Italian on the next call to the ground: 'Buona sera', and at the end of the exchange, 'Grazie'. Clive Elton then goes on the BA company frequency, telling the

BA staff in Rome, among other things, what the arrival time will be, and how much fuel is to be loaded for the return to London.

'Speedbird Rome. This is Speedbird 504.'

'Speedbird 504, good afternoon. Go ahead.'

'504, we are estimating on the stand at 1715 with a fit aircraft. We shall need 12 600 kilos of fuel for the return flight to London.'

BA Rome acknowledges, then asks that the passenger in seat Alpha 4 should be requested to contact ground staff on arrival. 'Tell him it is nothing special.' The captain acknowledges, then picks up the internal telephone and asks one of the stewardesses back in the cabin to pass the message on to the – slightly surprised – occupant of seat A4. 'Tell him it's nothing serious,' he adds.

Kilo Delta is tracking across northern Italy at 450 knots, Mach 0.79, 520 mph, still at 37 000 feet, with 220 miles to run to Rome and 100 miles to the beginning of the descent. The computer is forecasting a landing weight on Fiumicino's runway 16 Left of 78.1 tonnes. As the time to descend approaches, the crew asks for permission to leave flight level 37 zero and is given 15 zero. The computer is given the go-ahead, and right on the dot the throttles move themselves gently back, as if a ghost hand is upon them. The subdued roar of the engines softens. The nose of Kilo Delta dips.

'Speedbird 504 leaving three seven zero for one five zero.'

'Roger Speedbird 504.'

Approaching 15 000 feet the Italian air traffic controller is back on the radio. 'Speedbird 504, descend to eight thousand and hold.'

It is the first indication that there could be delays going into Rome, where such problems are not unknown. Captain Elton queries. 'Speedbird 504; how long the delay please?'

'Speedbird 504; not more than ten minutes.'

Kilo Delta continues to slant down, and at 12 000 feet leaves the blue sky to plunge into solid cloud cover. Rain streaks the windshield; unsettled air bounces the aircraft as if it is running fast over cobblestones. The weather is a total contrast to the tourist vision of sunny Italy.

ATC comes on to clear the flight down a further 2000 feet, but then comes the anticipated hold. 'Speedbird 504; make it a 360.'

'Speedbird 504; 360, thank you.'

EFIS is programmed, and the track on the video screen begins to show KD performing a wide circle over the Tarquinia holding point. But the bad news is followed almost at once by good.

'Speedbird 504, cleared for standard approach.'

Clive Elton acknowledges, and then goes on the PA to tell the passengers the current situation. 'Just a little delay . . . we had one twizzle over Tarquinia, but we are now commencing our descent and approach without further delay . . . Landing in just about ten minutes from now.'

Phil Bright is flying Kilo Delta down through 5000 feet, the clouds even greyer. Clive Elton, who will be the handling pilot for the landing, says he will do a manual touchdown (the roles will be reversed on the return leg, with the co-pilot doing the take-off and landing and the captain handling the cruise). The seat-belt signs are switched on in the cabin, and the cabin staff begin their pre-landing safety announcements. 'Seats upright . . . tables stowed away . . . fasten your seat belts . . . no smoking until after landing.' Once again, the entreaty is repeated in Italian.

On the flight-deck the workload is rising as KD buffets down through 4000 feet. The CSD opens the cockpit door and reports, 'All secure, captain.' The captain tells him, 'It's going to be windy, so tell the crew at the back end to strap themselves down.' John Hancock goes to relay the message.

At 3000 feet the flaps go out. There is still no sight of the ground. Clive Elton is on the radio. 'Speedbird 504, ten miles for 16 Left.'

'Speedbird 504, roger; you are number one to land.'

There are glimpses of the green and brown Roman landscape at 2400 feet. The wheels go down with a rumble at 2100 feet; speed brakes are armed, so that on landing they will automatically deploy as ground spoilers.

'504; outer marker.'

'504, roger. You are clear to land.'

Runway 16 Left comes into sight dead ahead through the murky after-noon when the aircraft is at 900 feet. The co-pilot takes her down, then at 200 feet, the height at which the decision is made either to land or climb away, he hands over to Clive Elton. 'I have control,' the captain confirms. The wind is 15 knots, gusting up to 25, straight down the runway.

Phil Bright calls out the heights as the runway lights begin to flash past each side. 'One hundred . . . fifty . . thirty.'

There is the slightest of jolts as Kilo Delta's undercarriage kisses the tarmac, then a blast of reverse thrust, helping the auto-braking system and the spoilers, which have popped up out of the wings, presses passengers and crew gently against their seat belts. The aircraft slows quickly, and turns off the active runway. So vast is Fiumicino that the crew have to tell the tower that they have cleared the runway. Charts are consulted as Kilo Delta taxies in to identify the whereabouts of the stand which has been allocated.

As the aircraft approaches the terminal building, the passengers for the return flight to London can be seen sitting behind the glass of the gateroom. Italian airport workers, in green overalls, come out to meet KD, shielding their ears against the 211s, one hauling a set of chocks for the under-carriage.

The engines are silenced, and the shutdown checks begin.

'Park brake?' 'Set.'

'Fuel control?' 'Cut off.'

'Hydraulic systems?' 'Set.'

'Fuel system?' 'Off.'

'Passenger signs?' 'Seat belts off.'

'Air conditioning system?' 'Set.'

It is the last of a total of nine checks which have been carried out between captain and co-pilot during the course of the service, five on the ground before take-off, three in the air, and one after landing. The words are kept to an absolute minimum, and the BA ethos is to make sure that actions to which the checks refer have already been taken – rather than to do them as the checks are sung out.

The steps are pushed up to the aircraft. The doors have been returned to manual, on orders from the flight-deck, and the main one is swung open. The passengers begin to disembark, each one given a farewell by John Hancock and his crew. In the cockpit captain and co-pilot get down to a last bit of paperwork. The computer shows that between Heathrow and Fiumicino the aircraft has used 8400 kilos of fuel, which is 500 kilos more than predicted before departure, due to the long initial hold at 27 000 feet, the short hold during the descent, and a long approach.

'Well, that's the easy bit finished,' says Clive Elton, and he and Phil Bright climb out of their seats to stretch their legs briefly at the aircraft door, before preparing for the return to London.

CHAPTER ELEVEN

COMPUTERISATION: FUTURE POWER
ON A PIN'S HEAD

In the days BC (before computers), the airlines used to take their bookings over the telephone, or via Telex, and clerks in a big room at headquarters would manually enter the current availability of each flight on boards up against the far wall. This system worked smoothly during the era of the DC-3, with thirty seats, and even the Britannia with two and a half times that number; but when the age of mass transport by jet was heralded in the early 1960s, with the entry into service of the new Boeing 707 and Douglas DC-8, offering up to 150 seats each flight, the system started to strain at the seams. BA men with long memories tell the story, and swear that it is true, that as passenger numbers multiplied and the reservations centre at BOAC was expanded to try to keep pace, clerks stationed in the back rows brought binoculars to work with them so that they could see the status boards.

Today, BA flies an average of 68 000 passengers a day – well over two million a month in the peaks of August and September – on 559 flights and 637 sectors. Computer technology arrived just in time to save the burgeoning airline industry from descending into a state of chaos, or at least from having its proper development severely limited by the sheer inability of the traditional systems to cope with rapidly accelerating numbers. Airlines in the United States, and notably American Airlines with its own system, coded SABRE (Semi-Automated Business Research Environment), had pioneered CRS (computer reservations systems), but BEA was the first carrier to introduce one in Europe. Its BEACON system went on line in 1965, based on the then Univac company's hardware and software, with BOAC following in 1968 with its IBM-designed BOADICEA. Of the two sister airlines, BOAC had the more complicated task in establishing a CRS for the long-haul intercontinental market, with stations as far away as New Zealand, South Africa and Japan, and with two, sometimes even three, identical flight numbers in the air at the same time because of the lengthy flight times involved. Those early airline computer pioneers were brave men, for they were moving into very high-risk territory with few charts, and with systems which were, by today's standards, amazingly rudimentary. They also had the uphill task of convincing traditional airline managements of the true worth of their 'new-fangled' devices, and that they were not going to lose the airlines all records of all their bookings in one big puff of smoke (the early systems did go down fairly regularly, but nothing of a catastrophic nature ever occurred).

The ubiquitous VDU, the visual display screen, on which information from the computer is brought up today at the touch of a key, was not available when the first computers came in to BEA. The procedure then was for a passenger or travel agent to ring the airline to enquire whether seats were available on a certain flight. The reservations clerk would then access the computer and the information would come back as a print-out, to be read down the phone to the enquirer. Gradually both airlines extended the range of their CRS systems, so that by the time of the merger into British Airways at the beginning of the 1970s, virtually the entire network had come on line. Such systems had to rely on excellent communications links, and here the management of the two airlines were fortunate in the foresight of their predecessors in having established such links in the years before and immediately after World War 2. Working with partner airlines in the old British Empire such as Trans Canada, South African Airways and Qantas, Imperial Airways and then BOAC had established a vital web of cables, and the OFTS network (Overseas Fixed Telecommunications System) still provides a common linkage around those countries – although satellite communications also pay an increasingly important part today. On routes where communications traffic is always particularly heavy, such as transatlantic, BA has its own privately-leased lines.

Seen in retrospect, the fact that BEA and BOAC developed two totally separate computer systems during the 1960s can be termed a nonsense; it was a point picked up by the committee under Sir Ronald Edwards which looked into the state of British civil air transport in May 1969, which recommended that the two should get together. Separate systems were a reflection that although BEA and BOAC were both British flag-carriers, both state-owned, the airlines played totally different roles in the short/medium-haul and long-haul markets, had differing computer needs, and were run as separate entities by fiercely independent managements. There is no doubt that there was an enormous amount of duplicated effort, and also an immense rivalry which effectively short-circuited any attempts to link BEACON and BOADICEA systems. When the BOAC/BEA merger came, computers were first in line to come together, but there were delicate decisions to be made as to which of the two systems should be used as the foundation for BA's new one – BABS, British Airways Business System. BOADICEA was eventually chosen, mainly on grounds that it was cheaper to convert it to handle short/medium-haul than it was to convert BEACON to handle long-haul – although it could have been done. It was also considered that IBM's architecture for airline systems, upon which BOADICEA was based, was going to be more of a standard throughout the industry in the years ahead. In retrospect, it was a correct decision, but at the time, when management feathers were already badly ruffled as the two airlines went through the painful process of sinking their identities into the newly-born BA, it upset a lot of people, and some left because of it.

What emerged was one of the largest and most sophisticated computer and communications systems in the world, servicing not only BA but some fifty third-party airline customers, from which deals BA made, and still makes, a considerable annual income. However, the early 1970s were still pioneering days for airline computerisation, with its 24 hours a day 365 days a year operational requirements, and the switching of BEACON and then BOADICEA into BABS, without the loss of a moment's business, was a demanding task. VDUs had been introduced by BOAC in 1967, five years before the merger (BEA followed suit in 1971). Giving the airline's staff throughout the world the ability to see the myriad information held in the computer back in London was a major breakthrough, and the management began to have a true concept of the worth of this 'sleeping giant' and the ways in which it could help BA embark on a successful future.

Today, BA has some 20 000 computer terminals in its entire network, plus over 1800 personal computers and 3500 office automation terminals in 750 locations worldwide. If those used by travel agencies and others to link into BABS are included, the total rises to well in excess of 100 000. So universal has the computer now become that very few of the airline's 48 000 employees, whether they are senior managers or pilots, check-in girls or chefs in the catering bases, will go through their working day without accessing it, or using in some way a segment of the information which it contains. By 1988 the BABS system was handling in the region of three million transactions each day (a transaction being every time the 'enter' key is pressed on a keyboard to demand a piece of information); the peak load on the computer ran into hundreds of demands every second, compared with the peak load elsewhere in industry of between one and five demands per second. How much information is held in the computer, how much 'data on line' is there? In answer to that sort of question people in BA tend to talk in gigabytes (each gigabyte is a thousand million characters and there are 403.3 gigabytes in BA's two main computers), and to cite the massive piles of London telephone directories (20 165 volumes in all) which would be required if the whole lot were to be printed out (and this store of information grows 30% a year). For although the original reservations use still generates the largest activity, BABS has a great variety of other tasks today, and BA will lean upon 'her' even more heavily in the future to do even more jobs.

BABS is, in fact, just one of many computer systems in operation today at two BA data centres at Heathrow airport. BABS drives passenger reservations, fares calculation, ticketing, check-in, and tour operations. A cargo service system looks after load reservations and consignment control, an operations system after flight planning, ops control, aircraft defect control, airport information and load control, and a further system after services for other airlines. Then there are systems for purchasing and supply, for ground transport, for aircraft engineering and maintenance, for human resources, for catering, for finance and accounting, and for planning scheduling resource control.

Tailor-made programmes have been designed as computerisation, or Information Management as it is now called, has developed in BA, enabling all the major departments to keep track of their own particular business or solve their own particular problems. These sub-operations can access each other through the central data banks so that if, for instance, a flight is delayed for whatever reason anywhere in the world, all the departments which such a delay will affect will be privy to the details, and can amend plans accordingly. BA's catering department, for instance, uses the computer facility in various ways – for production control to ensure that correct amounts of foodstuffs, beverages and all the other items which go on to every flight (36 000 separate items in the case of a 747) are purchased; for real-time control of the number of meals to be loaded for each flight – and for the different classes of accommodation in those flights – as passenger reservations fluctuate up and down right up to minutes before the aircraft doors are finally closed; for streamlining paperwork; and for checking contractors' charges.

Operations control uses computers to make sure that the right airliner, with the right crew and the right catering, is ready at the right place at the right time, and to keep an overall watch on the progress of all the sectors which the airline performs every day throughout the world. When a problem occurs, BABS or her friends will tell ops the implications. Those in the airline responsible for crew scheduling use computers both short- and long-term, to make sure that BA's pilots and engineers are deployed efficiently on the day, and also to forecast how many the airline will need up to five years ahead, taking into account the projected expansion of the business and the long lead time needed to recruit and train such staff. Engineering uses computers for, among other things, inventory control of its stocks of expensive spares – some 400 000 altogether – with the history of every part of every aircraft in the fleet, and whether it is in use, in stock, or under repair, listed in detail.

Computerisation has also been employed since the early 1980s for a highly sophisticated system of what is known as yield control, that is the maximising of the price at which every seat on every flight is sold. In the airline industry it is considered that those carriers which manage their yields correctly are the ones which will see the biggest future profits. Every airline has been conscious of this truism in the past, but computerisation has given them a tool to make it work. In simple terms, the trick is to fine-tune the sales operation for every service so that seats are not unloaded on to the discount market – and which could then find their way into the bucket shops – which might sell at a later stage to the business market at a far higher price. But conversely, if seats which could be sold at a discount are held back for the business market, and the business people do not mater-ialise, they go empty – and there are few products as perishable as an airline seat. Unlike tins of beans on the supermarket shelf, if they do not sell today they can't be sold tomorrow. Forecasting what the demand is going to be up to 365 days ahead really needs a crystal ball, but the BA computer is able to do it with some certainty when fed a wide range of data – what the trend of bookings has been on that same flight in the past, whether there are any special events going on at either end of the route (the France–England rugby internationals always produce a surge of travel on Heathrow–Paris flights, for instance), and many other factors which could affect who is going to travel, and on what sort of ticket. The customer is unaware of all this going on behind the BA scenes; he or she meets up with computeri-sation when ringing the airline, or a travel agent, for a seat, or perhaps for cargo space, and when a positive answer comes back within the space of seconds. Members of the BA Executive Club (£125 a year membership, with the use of special lounges at airports, travel insurance, discount car hire and hotel rates, and other benefits) simply have to give their club number when booking; the computer knows who they are, and even where they like to sit on the aircraft – smoking or non-smoking, window or aisle.

When the passenger goes to the BA sales desk at the airport to pay for and collect his ticket, the Departure Control System (DCS) computer prints it out for him, finds him the right seat, prints his boarding card, and updates the number of people who have checked in for the flight so that those responsible for moving it away from the gate on time will know precisely how many who booked have arrived, and how many are going to move into the group which no airline really knows how to handle, the 'no-shows'. Yield management is becoming increasingly clever at forecasting what the no-show rate is going to be for any given flight on any particular day (up to 2.5 bookings can sometimes be taken for each seat), but if the computer forecast is wrong BA could find itself oversold, with angry passengers banging the desk and vowing to take their business to a competitor in the future. The no-show rate can be as much as 40%, especially for business flights on Fridays; but the average is between 10 and 12%, and BA allows for 8%. The computer also holds the serial numbers of stolen tickets, although the first line of defence against this type of fraud continues to be the sharp eyes of the ground staff at the check-in. DCS can also make aircraft weight and balance calculations and will, in the future, print bag tags. From the early days when computers were viewed with some suspicion, the whole vast and growing area of information technology is now generally accepted within BA, even by most of the generation which went through school and into business well before computers became the everyday and vital aids that they are to many people today.

A real problem is to keep management abreast with the fast-moving developments in this field, and to this end BA's Information Technology department gives monthly briefings, bringing in some of the best-known computer 'gurus' as lecturers. The airline also has a computer programme called AIMS (airline information management systems), to which the top 180 in BA have access, which offers a wealth of otherwise highly confidential business information in both word and graph form. The information includes how the bookings went the previous day, how they compared with previous sales, area-to-area sales breakdowns, whether budgets are being hit. On Tuesday mornings a guide to the airline's revenue performance the previous week becomes available on the screens on some management desks – AIMS offers what is known as a hierarchy of data, activated through a series of passwords, so that only the top echelons receive, for instance, information on profitability.

In all, AIMS offers a choice of thiry-five menus covering information on BA, its competitors, and the current economic state of the world. Sir Colin Marshall is an information-technology enthusiast and an avid user of the pearls which the system has to offer – a fact which has encouraged his managers, even those who were originally stricken with what is known as 'techno-terror', to take it seriously and utilise it. The Chief Executive generally has three monitor screens working around his desk in BA's Heathrow headquarters – AIMS, BA's pages on Oracle, and the FIND monitor, which is driven by the main Flight Information and Control (FICO) system, the latter two offering a detailed and up-to-the-second rundown on how the airline's services all over the world are performing.

AIMS played an important role in helping BA to work its way successfully out of the potentially catastrophic economic situation produced by the twin events of Chernobyl fall-out and the Libyan bombing within days of each other in April 1986. On its screens BA's managers were given daily briefings as bookings cancellations by nervous would-be tourists to Europe began to overtake new reservations during a period which is normally a peak booking time of year. AIMS' sophisticated modelling forecasts of the way the traffic could be expected to develop over the rest of that summer helped management decide that an intensive marketing campaign in the United States, rather than desperate fares discounting, was going to be the answer. And so it proved.

BA now has 1800 employees working in information technology, or around one in twenty-five of its staff, which indicates the seriousness with which the whole business is taken within the airline. Around 800 of these work on the operational side, 800 on the development of new systems, and 200 in support and planning. The airline now spends some 3½% of its annual revenue on investment in information management, and this compares with 1½% only five years previously. By 1992 the proportion is expected to be 5%. These figures include amortisation and depreciation of the assets, for with the galloping pace of the sector, BA reckons to write off computers in five years, personal computers over three, and telecoms over seven. Hardware in use at any time is worth around £100 million. The value of the software is really incalculable, because it has taken 5000 *man-years* to accumulate and is therefore virtually irreplaceable. Which leads to the obvious question – what happens if, due to some disaster, the whole system goes down, wiping off all the records and leaving BA totally informationless? The answer is that such a happening has been made virtually impossible. Copies of all the data held in the system are taken every twenty-four hours and are stored in different places, including a fire-proof safe. BA looks for, and obtains, 99.6% availability around the clock, using a back-up system which includes stand-by computers which automatically switch in, the airline's own power station, with flywheels which smooth out surges in the current and diesels which cut in if there is a break, stringent fire precautions, and the tightest security. The airline also has this whole area of its business covered with a huge insurance. Because of these precautions, and the need to keep going night and day right round the year, operational costs are probably at least double those of computer operations in other industries.

It is a sector of the airline where progress is breathtaking, where there is reckoned to be a tenfold improvement in technology every ten years, and where the price becomes cheaper and the equipment becomes smaller at a pace to take the breath away. John Watson, BA's Director of Information Management, forecast:

> Virtually everybody in BA within the next five years will have to use a computer at some time in their day-to-day job, in addition to the high percentage of our staff who use them now. But people are becoming more familiar with this technology in their everyday lives; their children use it as a matter of course. As an airline, we have got to do this to survive. In the 1960s and 1970s, people in our sector of the business were looked upon as a race apart, the technocrats, the back-room boys, but now everybody has to use information technology, even if they don't understand what makes it work. It's like knowing how to drive a car and not how to repair it. Our strategic thrust must be to educate our managers in IT, to produce a cultural change, for the companies that are going to be successful in the future are the ones which get their managers to be systems- and technology-

aware, and which get their technologists to be business-aware. Some of our people are still frightened of computers, but it is a lot less than it used to be.

If we hadn't had computers, there is no doubt that the marvels of commercial air transport would not have been realised, because we would not have been able to utilise the hardware – the aeroplanes that cost the money – to the degree that we have to utilise them to encourage the growth of air transport. What computers have done for British Airways is to give us the ability to handle the vast numbers of people who want to fly, to handle the logistics of the scale of the operation, and to handle it all on an economic level that enables the fares to come down – which, in turn, fires the growth.

BA is channelling a lot of its information-technology expertise and funds for the near-term future into the Galileo computer reservations consortium, of which it was a founder member. Other members include Aer Lingus, Alitalia, Austrian Airlines, KLM, Olympic, Sabena, Swissair, TAP Air Portugal and United Airlines' Covia, the computer reservations system of United Airlines. Galileo has its headquarters at Swindon, in Wiltshire, England, and went on line in 1988–9 after the airline members had put in a total of $200 million to establish it. The cost of its operation is likely to run to several hundred millions of dollars a year. The consortium has its own computer complex, with lines into its member airlines' own computers, including BABS at Heathrow, and offers travel agents a very wide selection of travel information – flights, car hire, hotel accommodation, train, bus and shipping services, resorts, weather trends, theatres and other entertainment. Galileo was established to make the offering of such a wealth of information possible, to share the formidable costs involved, and to keep the giant United States carriers, the 'mega-airlines' as they are called, which were already big in this sector in their own country, from spreading their systems into the European patch. John Watson said, 'We recognised in British Airways that in the future airlines have got to have control over the distribution of their products and services. The idea is not to replicate what we have today, but to build on its strengths, and to obtain a capability to control the electronic marketplace.'

Shared systems can also bring down operating costs dramatically. The cost of booking a ticket from a travel agent through BA's centralised telephone reservations system is around £6, plus commission, whereas the cost of making that booking through a computerised reservations system, such as Travicom which is in the travel agent's office, is around £2. SABRE and Apollo, the two giant American computer reservations systems, cost an estimated $1.80 per passenger sector.

Information technology in BA has come a very long way in a relatively short time. Thirty years ago, a booking query from Sydney to London would chatter laboriously over the Telex, be dealt with manually, and then be transmitted back down the line. Today, that same question takes pre-

cisely two seconds to flash to London, be answered by BABS, and be back on
the VDU in Australia; a complicated routing involving, say, thirty-six
sectors would take a little longer, perhaps five seconds. What will the IT
scene be like by the turn of the century? John Watson: 'Computing power
which ten years ago required a space the size of a tennis court needs space the
size of a tennis ball today, and in ten years' time may go on a pin-head.
Perhaps that goes some way towards answering the question?'

CHAPTER TWELVE

A GLANCE INTO THE CRYSTAL BALL

Forecasting the future in the world of civil aviation is a notoriously uncertain business, given the ease with which the industry can be knocked off course by factors well outside its control – macroeconomics, fluctuations in currencies, world standards of living influencing business and leisure travel patterns, the price of oil, environmental pressures, wars or rumours of wars. But airlines – and BA is certainly no exception – have to make an attempt at it so that they can gain at least an idea of what their short-, medium- and long-term capital investment patterns might be for the massive variety of items which they require to run the business – items ranging from human resources to bricks and mortar, from terminal space to aircraft capacity.

What new airliners to acquire, and when, is the recurring conundrum for any airline. Having too few, or too many, at a particular time could produce red ink on the annual balance sheet and, in the very worst case, financial ruin. BA has taken care of this problem in the short/medium term through its policy of leasing rather than buying outright, but what of the long term? Will the airliners of the early years of the next century be bigger than they are now, smaller, fatter, thinner, jet-powered, unducted fan-powered, hydrogen-powered, nuclear-powered, even powered by the rays of the sun? Will BA passengers bound for Australia in the year 2050 climb aboard a space ship at a space station (not Heathrow – the noise would be too overwhelming) and arrive overhead Sydney in under an hour, including a short time in orbit?

The manufacturers of aerospace hardware obviously have a deep vested interest in the answers to such rarefied questions, and each does its forecast of the numbers of new airliners which the world will require in twenty-five years' time. Boeing's 1988 look into that sort of future came up with a requirement for 7464 jet aircraft, worth a total of $342 billion, of which sum $100 billion will be for replacement aircraft and $242 billion to take care of growth requirements. When a further $72 billion-worth of jet airliners already ordered but not delivered was added on, the grand total to 2005 came to $414 billion – or just twice what it was during the previous 17-year period, 1970–87.

Boeing based its optimistic view of the future on assumptions of declining airline costs and air fares, low fuel prices, the introduction of new technology and automation, lower real-labour costs, the increase in tourism and less regulation by governments, a modest growth in the world economy (giving continuing growth in discretionary income to be spent on travel), stable or even lower interest rates, minimal inflation, increased employment, and no major recessions. Travel, Boeing believed, would grow at a moderate 5% per year through to 2005 – meaning that the 1988 market would double in size by the year 2000, and reach two and a half times by 2005. During the 1990s airliners would become bigger – 'dramatically' was the word Boeing used. From 1994 to 2005 more than three-quarters of the seats delivered would be in aircraft with more than 240 seats, a trend which would be driven by the need to minimise airport congestion, and to cope with growing market size, increased range requirements, and the demand for better airliner economics. After 1994 airliners with more than 350 seats would account for 46% of all aircraft delivered.

BA takes the annual Boeing glimpse into the future seriously, particularly as it is today largely a Boeing operator. But its Planning Department looks also at many other prognostications – from manufacturers, from the international aviation organisations, from private financial and economic institutions, and from a wide variety of other sources. Everybody has their own view as to what rate the business will grow between now and the next millennium. BA's thinking is based on an assumption of something between 4½% and 6% per year compound, covering both the scheduled and charter markets, with the growth at the lower end of that range in the shorter term. There are indeed a lot of people out there who have never set foot on an aeroplane in their lives – even in relatively sophisticated areas of the world such as Europe and the United States the proportion of those who have flown reaches only 12%. Airlines have learned to be highly suspicious of sweeping forecasts by economists that rising standards of living in countries like China and Brazil are going to produce an 'explosion' of air travel in the near term. Both China and Brazil are in the process of building up aerospace industries of their own, but when their teeming populaces will begin to climb aboard the products of these industries in more than the present penny numbers is impossible to guess, even to the nearest decade.

Of more immediate interest to BA and the other major world airlines are the various forces which they identify as having the ability to restrain their reasonable growth. Such forces include ATC and airport constraints, increasingly tight regulations covering aircraft noise and other forms of pollution, competition from improving forms of surface transport, and competition from new methods of global communication as the digital/electronics revolution takes off.

Airports' and airways' congestion is already having an impact on BA's flights into, out of and across Europe, and this situation is likely to become worse rather than better in the future. Flow control – the limiting of the number of flights despatched and received during any one hour – was introduced during peak flying months in the south-east of England by the middle 1980s, not necessarily because the skies over that area were dangerously congested, but because of the knock-on effect of delays as flights are filtered across the many national airspaces of Europe. The dream of one international ATC authority covering all the countries of the continent, as is the case in the United States, has not been realised, and does not look like being realised in the foreseeable future. Meanwhile, each nation has its own control system operating its own equipment, with its own controllers with their own trade union practices operating to their own standards. Europe is the classic aviation crossroads, with streams of traffic going north–south, and east–west. It is also riddled with areas blocked off for military flying, which cause the airways to take dog-leg bends, so forcing up the fuel burn. At the centre of the European crossroads lies West Germany, and it surprised nobody in the airline business to hear Lufthansa report that during 1988 its airliners spent a total of 10 000 hours in holding patterns over Frankfurt, Munich and Dusseldorf, costing the airline some $50 million extra outlay.

According to the grand design of the European Commission, the aviation frontiers of Europe are to be swept away by 1992, giving all airlines in the Community the right to fly where they like, when they like, at what fares they wish to charge. Whether such a radical reform will actually happen by that date is doubted by most airline managers, but a measure of liberalisation has been happening in Europe for some years as a lead-in to the reform. Britain has signed new and liberalised bilateral air-service agreements with several of its EEC partners, notably Holland and Eire. Such agreements are throwing new traffic into the air, but the new traffic is not being matched by improvements to the infrastructure through which it flies and on which it takes off and lands. One BA manager commented, 'As far as the politicians are concerned, there are votes in cheap fares, but no votes in building new airports.'

The airline came out strongly during 1989 in favour of a liberalised aviation industry for Europe. A muscular manifesto was issued, trumpeting:

We say civil aviation should not wait for 1992. Set the airlines free now. Liberalisation throughout the European Community will bring benefits to the whole community. British Airways urges an open market, with the customer as the judge. We wholeheartedly welcome competition, because the market grows under the stimulus of competition. Freedom to set innovative fares, and offer as much capacity – the number of flights and seats as the market demands – would spread across Europe the benefits already proved to exist in the free civil aviation markets that some of the EC states already have with Britain. Multi-designation of airlines instead of restricting a route to one airline from each country, and the freedom to carry passengers from any EC country to any other EC country, should come sooner rather than later.

Britain, the manifesto points out, is alone in having a competely private-sector aviation industry, with all the others either partly or wholly nationalised. 'The freedom to compete is a cornerstone of the Treaty of Rome. Civil aviation needs a Europe-wide free market. This cannot come about while some national airlines remain state-controlled.' Airline competition, in BA's view, cannot be truly open and fair while some carriers are supported – or protected – by their national governments for 'out-dated nationalistic reasons', while others have to fend for themselves against competition from outside the Community.

BA sees the opportunities of the Common Air Transport Policy as the ultimate stage of liberalisation, in setting the airlines free from bureaucratic constraints and letting the customer reap the benefits of competition. The airlines would be able to operate as other industries do, within normal trading legislation within the European Community.

The package of liberalisation measures must ensure that safety and fair competition would be maintained in aviation, as in all other fields of industry.

Except for safety issues – best left to national authorities – the airline's view is that a single level of regulation is needed from Brussels, 'not an extra layer of bureaucracy on top of the existing governmental agencies'. Only in that way could extra cost be avoided, and compliance assured by all member states and their airlines in liberalisation. Pricing freedom, in BA's view, is particularly important, so that there can be response to the needs of the market place.

The airline is also keen on moves towards harmonisation of European time zones, favouring the adoption of GMT plus one hour throughout the winter, with double summer time in summer. The benefits to business are, it believes, well documented, while the benefits to tourism are every bit as important. 'What about getting Europe and the USA into step on the dates on which we change our clocks? And what about moving one of the British Spring Bank holidays such as May Day to, say, the end of October, and help create a longer season that way?'

But BA also warns in its manifesto that much of the planned harmonisation threatens to undo hard-won benefits in fares and services already achieved. Bringing Britain into line with VAT on transport will be one such retrograde step, the airline pleads.

> There is no VAT on air travel in Britain. It would be an irony if at a time when the airlines are striving to reduce fares, external presssures to add to costs simply as bureaucratic tidying-up were suddenly to be applied. Civil aviation is different from any other industry. It is truly international, and an air ticket is far more negotiable and more acceptable than virtually any other piece of paper, currency included.
>
> A passenger can buy a ticket in Alaska for travel between London and Edinburgh. Where would the VAT element of that fare be paid? And what would be payable on a ticket from Manchester to non-EC Switzerland, and then on to Italy or Greece? Would a non-EC intercontinental airline pay VAT on a European sector, and to whom? Will the existing definition of an international journey remain? And who would police such complexities? VAT on European airlines' ticket sales would introduce new market distortions and anomalies, just at a time when we should be removing old ones.

BA is also mightily concerned over EC plans to do away with duty-free sales on routes between EC countries. The airline's view is that when duty-free goes, air fares – and Channel ferry fares – will inevitably go up. Duty-free sales, it argues, make a substantial contribution to airport revenues, while many charter airlines derive revenue from on-board duty-free sales, which have kept the price of travel down. A further retrograde step seen by BA is the imposition of bureaucratic procedures designed to ensure that the public sector does not purchase only in their national markets. This proposal, it considers, is irrelevant to airlines operating in a highly-competitive international field. 'EC public procurement rules would impose significant delays, and costs, on British Airways as on other airlines.' And the obligation to make public all but the most minor purchasing requirements would be a gift of sensitive commercial information to the competition outside the EC, notably to the United States and Japan.

Regulation on pay and working conditions should be kept to a minimum, the airline believes. Wages and employment conditions should be determined by the practices in each member state. Any harmonisation in this area can only be artificial, inasmuch as it ignores local labour market conditions, and it will increase prices and restrict genuine competition. BA's European manifesto inquires,

> 'Who in Brussels is in a position to dictate to a commuter airline operating in, say, Greece, what it should pay its pilots? How can EC airlines compete on a global basis and adapt new challenges if they are ossified in harmonised labour costs and practices?'

When all European Community travel becomes domestic travel, questions such as national ownership of airlines, controls on which airline can go on which routes, restrictions on the number of flights each airline is allowed to operate, will no longer have much significance for the airlines, and their passengers. In the airline's view,

> We seek the freedom to price our services in Europe freely in a competitive market so as to capture their value as perceived by customers. Many countries outside the EC already fear 'Fortress Europe', and in seeking to gain footholds in the Community, will try to play us off against each other. Over-protection of the weak, by denying growth opportunities to their home-market competitors, never helped the strong remain strong enough to fight the global competition. There is no doubt that the airlines, like other industries, are better off in the tough competitive world than they are when safely insulated by government support. The consumer is certainly better off too.

On the air traffic control situation in Europe too, BA is in favour of national operations giving way to a co-ordinated pan-European system of managing the airways. The technology exists, it believes. Investment in ATC is vital if the philosophy of 'one Europe' is to be a reality. 'There must be a balance between the needs of the traveller and the protection of the environment. Airports are essential. The airlines have invested massively in new-technology, quieter, cleaner aircraft. The politics of the environment should recognise the realities, and the practicalities.'

From BA's point of view, the development of Heathrow Airport, its main base (although the second London airport at Gatwick assumed increased importance following the BCal takeover), is crucial for the future. Not only does the airline have a vast investment in buildings and equipment, including its main engineering centre, operations centre, catering bases, and corporate headquarters at Heathrow, but the airport is also an essential interline point into which passengers are fed by the short/medium-haul network to be captured by the long-haul flights. By the middle 1980s Heathrow was saturated at peak periods, despite the opening of the new fourth terminal on the southern perimeter, into which BA transferred all its intercontinental services plus a few short-hauls. Where to go for the future? The obvious direction is to the western boundary of the airport where there is a large site lying between the two main east–west runways, occupied by the Perry Oaks sewage-disposal works.

Both Heathrow Airport Ltd (HAL) and BA want to see the Perry Oaks site – which at around 300 acres is as big as the whole central area of the airport with its three terminals – developed as a new terminal, on grounds that what Heathrow is short of is not runway capacity (aircraft are getting bigger, and whatever its size an airliner generally spends no more than 60 seconds actually occupying the concrete during take-off or landing), but terminal capacity (it is estimated that each passenger spends on average a total of one hour passing through the terminals before leaving, and after arriving). HAL envisages the Perry Oaks terminal as being big enough to handle up to 30 million passengers a year. This is a massive project indeed, particularly when it is remembered that Terminal 4 at Heathrow, the new north terminal at Gatwick and the new terminal at Stansted airport could just about take this annual total between them.

Developing Perry Oaks will be a lengthy affair, with the planning application, likely to go in during 1990, bound to be 'called in' by the government, so that it will be subject to a public planning inquiry. Such an inquiry is not likely to last less than a year, and then there will be a further six months at least while the inquiry inspector prepares his report. Assuming that this report is favourable towards the project, it is estimated that it will take up to five years to clear the site (the lagoons of which contain two and a half million tons of sludge), during which time an alternative site could be developed elsewhere. Building the new terminal would take at least two years, and so it could hardly be in operation much before the turn of the century. BA's ideal plan would be to move all of its Heathrow services to Perry Oaks, so releasing both Terminals 1 and 4, and giving the airline enormous economies in having a single-terminal operation, and making changing aircraft from long-haul to short-haul, and vice versa, simple – compared with the split operation which takes place today, that is. Passengers changing between BA flights and those of other airlines would still have to commute between terminals, but BA sees this as a factor in helping to keep travellers 'loyal' to it throughout their journeys. Whether HAL would allow BA to occupy such a new terminal exclusively is in some doubt. Past policies by HAL result in Aer Lingus, British Midland, and others, sharing Terminal 1 with BA, and KLM and Air Malta sharing Terminal 4. But BA will fight its corner on this issue and is prepared for a long campaign.

Based on its experience of having to shuttle between Terminals 1 and 4 at Heathrow, and between Heathrow and Gatwick, the last thing that BA wants is any further split in its operations in the south-east of the country. For this reason, the airline set its face against any proposal to push some of its services into Stansted, or to have more-distant airports, such as Manston, Lydd, or Bournemouth, developed as 'overflows' for the London area. BA sees its long-term future bound up with Heathrow, although it appreciates that it will have a stiff fight on its hands to convince the environmental movement that what it, and HAL, propose will not ruin the entire area for ever.

The case in favour of a terminal on the Perry Oaks site runs along these lines. Although its capacity would be 30 million passengers a year, it would not mean any more aircraft movements. There are two reasons for this: as stated earlier, airliners are becoming larger (BA estimate that the average load per aircraft landing at Heathrow will be 170 within five years instead of 117 as it was in 1989), and as a 'trade-off' for Perry Oaks, Terminal 2 in the central area of the airport would be demolished. Perry Oaks would therefore become the fourth terminal at the airport, rather than the (emotive) fifth. The site of the present Terminal 2, which was the first terminal to be developed in the central area after World War 2, would be used for extensions of existing facilities there, and in particular to provide better aircraft parking facilities. Now some forty years old, Terminal 2 is time-expired as a building, although the BAA did do its best to improve it over the years. Its design, and the concept of placing it on an island site in the middle of the runway complex, linked to the outside world by tunnels, was *avant garde* at that brave new time, but looks eccentric today. It is used by the foreign short/medium-haul airlines, who do not love it, particularly for the low ceilings over many of its check-in areas and for its general lack of room. Terminals 1 and 3, although more modern in design, also suffer from being on the island site.

Because no startling increases in the number of airliner movements are planned, and because the new generations of aircraft have engines far quieter than those which powered their predecessors, there should, the argument continues, be no increase in aircraft noise. The main impact on the environment would come from the increase in road traffic which the new fourth terminal would generate around the western end of the airport, part of which is green belt land. The developers' case is that this increase would be handled by new links to be built with the network of motorways which run near that end of Heathrow, the M25, the M4, and the M3, while the Heathrow Express train, with which HAL plans to link the Paddington rail terminus in central London with the airport, would have stations underneath each terminal, including the new one.

When it opens in late 1993 – supposing that the development timetable goes to plan – the Heathrow Express will carry six million passengers a year, with plenty of room to expand, so siphoning off a significant percentage of those who reach the airport by road. The fare, as projected in 1989, will be £6 single, over three times as expensive as the London Underground which also links central London to the Heathrow terminals, but the Heathrow Express trains will cover the journey to the central area terminals, non-stop, in only sixteen minutes, reaching a top speed of 100 mph.

HAL and British Rail (BR), joint developers of the Heathrow Express link, themselves ran into environmental objections. A House of Lords committee which, during early 1989, considered the Parliamentary Bill necessary for its setting-up, rejected the route of the spur into the airport which was to come off the main Paddington–West of England rail line at Hayes. The promoters then came up with an alternative route which dives into a tunnel shortly after coming off the main line, so passing beneath green belt land and the M4 motorway without any loss of agricultural land, with no need to demolish buildings, and with no visual or noise impact on nearby villages. This second plan, which also included the relocation of a lake for the benefit of wildlife, was being considered by Parliament in the opening months of 1990, and HAL and BR hope to begin work by the end of that year.

BA's plan, announced during 1989, to join up with two European airlines, KLM of Holland and Sabena of Belgium, could be viewed as a way of relieving the pressure on Heathrow and Gatwick. Under this plan, BA and KLM each acquired 20% in Sabena World Airways, a newly-created subsidiary of Sabena which holds the remaining 60%. All three carriers, while continuing to compete in other directions, will contribute to the creation of a major European hub at Brussels airport. BA passengers from UK provincial centres like Manchester and Birmingham wanting to inter-line with long-haul flights will be able to change aircraft at Brussels instead of first flying through London.

A further futuristic direction attempted by BA during 1989, but one which came to nothing, was its plan to take a $750 million, 15% stake in a $6.8 billion management and employee-led buy-out of the United States mega-airline, United. BA became involved through a mixture of defensive and opportunistic motives, the two airlines having, some time earlier, entered into an extensive marketing agreement under which they shared airport terminals, and provided connecting services between each other's flights. Sir Colin Marshall explained at the time the bid was launched:

> If it should fail, we can continue to do what we are doing now, provided the commercial agreement remains in place. But if United was acquired by a consortium including a Lufthansa, an Air France, or an Iberia, the commercial agreement would collapse, and we would be left scratching around to see what we can do to replace it.

Under the plan, Colin Marshall was to take a seat on the United board, while United's chief executive officer, Stephen Wolf, was to join BA's board as a non-executive director.

Progress was smooth in the early stages, and as the deal appeared to come together Lord King said expansively that it would 'allow two of the world's best airlines to develop alongside each other as the most formidable international partnership in every part of the globe,' adding, 'the investment will benefit our shareholders increasingly over the coming years'. BA's justification of its far-reaching plan was: an investment in the world's second-largest airline, with more than 400 aircraft, but for a price equivalent to six new jumbo jets; a foothold in the world's largest travel market, which accounted in 1988 for 39% of all scheduled air passengers – and which, by US law, BA could not currently freely service (United also provided the key to the fast-growing Pacific area, where it had bought Pan American's route network); route networks which fitted together perfectly, as far as BA's management was concerned, and which had further potential for development under the existing marketing agreement; a significant addition to BA's recent strategic acquisitions – British Caledonian, and the Sabena link which was being negotiated at that time; a share in United's future prosperity, which BA saw as considerable; and protection of BA's future against similar moves by its competitors.

First signs that all might not be well came from Washington DC, with the US government complaining that the proposed investment would give BA too much influence over the affairs of a US company. KLM, which was at that time seeking to take a $400 million stake in NWA, parent of another major US airline Northwest, fell victim to the same attitude, leading both European carriers to allege in private that what Washington was doing was to 'move the goalposts'. The issue went to diplomatic level, with the British embassy in Washington making the point to US officials that it was in the mutual interest of both countries for there to be as open and free an investment climate for outside investors as possible. And while the United pilots' union had agreed a contractual undertaking to accept lower wages and more efficient working practices – concessions estimated to be worth $250 million a year as a form of equity and collateral – the airline's machinists' union, representing the largest single group of employees, refused to make any similar concession, attacking the plan as 'insane'.

BA had no trouble raising the £320 million which it wanted through a rights issue with its shareholders, but then the whole deal edifice toppled and fell when the New York stock market lost faith one Friday in mid-October, marking United's shares down heavily and sparking off a temporary collapse in the Dow Jones index. There were rumours that the deal could be revived with finance from other sources, but BA wasted little time in pronouncing it dead. So the British airline withdrew its interest – officially 'stepping back to see how the US situation evolved,' and adding that there was no intention of participating in any United deal in the foreseeable future.

As the dust settled, there was speculation in the press about how the marketing agreement betweeen BA and UAL would stand the strains imposed by the failure of the investment deal, and also that a rift had emerged between Lord King and Sir Colin Marshall as a result of the collapse. Marshall, one of the deal's most enthusiastic advocates, had, the reports went, been in Tokyo trying to put together a financial package to save it, but had had the ground cut from beneath him by his chairman's decision to pull out. 'Rubbish,' growled Lord King. 'There are absolutely no tensions.'

Looking into the more distant future, BA, like the rest of the aviation industry, has considered the possibility of the one-million-lb weight airliner, with 560/600 seats for long-haul routes, perhaps in a double-deck configuration. But although totally feasible technically, infrastructure problems begin to look serious at this point, notably in accommodating the 250-foot enlarged wingspan of such super-jumbos on the aircraft stands and taxiways of a generation of airports designed and developed for an era when the Boeing 707 was considered to be the last word.

But will the travelling public always want to climb aboard airliners in the future – particularly as the post-war 'glamour' of air travel is now disappearing and the entire scene becomes increasingly crowded? BA is conscious of the growing attraction of some forms of surface transport, especially in the short-haul sector – from the high-speed train, sea ferry and hovercraft to the private motor car and the heavy goods vehicle. Over a number of years the airline has developed its own network of juggernaut trucks, operating to strict timetables and with aircraft-style flight numbers, which feed freight from cities in Europe into its cargo centre at Heathrow. Considerable planning time has been spent in working out the likely impact on its services, both within Britain and to the nearer European destinations – Paris or Brussels, for instance – of the opening of the Channel tunnel in 1992. Working with forecasts published in the prospectus of British Rail and SNCF French Railways, but without the benefit of vital details such as fare levels and journey times, BA envisages its loss of traffic on the short-haul routes from the south-east of England as running within a scale of 17–60%, constituting a loss of 1½–2 years' traffic growth – a hiccough, but a not unimportant hiccough at that. And depending upon the ease and attractiveness with which the public perceives the Chunnel after it has settled down into operation, traffic on the longer routes into Europe, to places like Geneva and Cologne, could be affected in the longer term. BA also sees possible compensations stemming from this 20-mile link which will finally do away with Britain's geographical insularity from her continental neighbours, such as package deals with the railways under which they bring leisure passengers through the tunnel from Europe to join the airline's flights out of Gatwick and Heathrow.

Leisure travel looms large in BA's forward thinking, for this sector provides three-quarters of its current business, and its future growth rate is predicted to be marginally larger than that in the business sector. Like most other people in the travel business, BA has noted the swift rise of socio-economic groups such as double-income parents whose children have left home, pensioners with savings to spare, professional men and women taking early retirement with generous golden handshakes, beneficiaries of inherited wealth, families with time and money on their hands as the working week contracts and robotisation and computerisation become increasingly common. The assumption within the airline is that the trend will be towards second holidays, and that one of those holidays will be taken at a long-haul destination rather than in Europe. Always depending on external factors like fluctuations in the exchange rate, big swings in traffic to areas such as the southern USA, South America and the Far East, Spain and Italy, are foreseen.

But while the vacationer taking advantage of discounted 'come-ons' will surge in numbers, is there any reason why the high-yield-fare business executive should not stay at home, given the ease with which he can do his work via satellite? Teleconferencing, in which groups of business people can see each other on screens set up in their offices, and can discuss projects, plans and ideas as if they were sitting together, is already a fact of corporate life; data zoom instantly from one side of the earth to the other; pictures of documents are on the desk 6000 miles away almost as soon as they are demanded. BA has noted a loss due to these trends of between 2–3% of its business traffic, but remains sanguine on the topic for the future, on the grounds that much business travel is anticipatory – you never know what business you may gain until you are actually there, that it is much more impressive in the eyes of a customer or potential customer if the vendor actually takes the trouble to go to see him personally, that there is no substitute for handshaking, for what is known as 'pressing the flesh', and that the sheer human desire to get out and about will never be suppressed. And there remains an inescapable suspicion that businessmen and businesswomen actually enjoy their business travel, despite all groanings and protestations to the contrary.

Vast improvements in in-flight communications are on their way, and can be seen as making the decision to go away from the office for a few days an easier one. In the past there has always been the fear of being out of touch while in transit, of being left out of the decision-making process, of not being available to speak to the important client when he appears without notice. Telephone calls from airliners flying over North America to numbers on the ground became commonplace in the early 1980s, and field experiments were going on successfully from airliners flying over long tracts of water towards the end of the decade. Calls from the ground to individuals in flight were due to follow soon after, and by the middle 1990s the airliner as a mobile workstation should be commonplace. Airbus Industrie demonstrated in Toulouse an airborne office in a mock-up of its A340 long-range airliner in which the business passengers would be able to telephone, Telex, use Fax, and generally be able to comport themselves much as they would be doing if in their offices on the ground. With sectors becoming longer and longer in the future as the aerodynamics of the airframe and the fuel consumption of jet engines improve further, airlines reason that their business travellers may wish to spend at least some of their time aloft – and 12/14-hour sectors will be commonplace on long-haul routes – actively engaged in their work rather than passing the time reading, dozing and being sustained.

Such offices in the sky will depend for their efficient working on good communications links, and BA demonstrated the feasibility of these with a decision in mid-1988 to spend £6 million on installing equipment to enable its Concorde, TriStar and Boeing737/757/747–200 fleets to transmit and receive instant messages, either automatically generated or entered through a keyboard. The system is used for operational control, maintenance and engine-health monitoring. By utilising it, BA's development engineers are able to determine the vibration level of an engine on an airliner flying a route thousands of miles away from the Heathrow base, without any need for action by the crew on board. The system is mainly used by BA Operations Control and Engineering, but it can also produce, on request, weather data. Pilots taking a service from Heathrow to Nice, for instance, are able to request a weather forecast for the Paris area and receive an automatic response in seconds.

What sort of aircraft will BA's future passengers be flying? The airline's planners spend a large proportion of their time looking for answers to this particular question, studying not only the individual aircraft which are either on offer or projected by aerospace manufacturers all over the world, but trends. Proposals by both Boeing and McDonnell Douglas for airliners powered by unducted fan engines sent a *frisson* through the entire airline industry in the early 1980s. Promised reductions of 30% in fuel use, up to 15% in seat-mile costs and 8% overall, could hardly be ignored, and BA was very disappointed when Boeing put its 7J7 project on the back-burner, particularly as the airline had done a lot of work with the US manufacturer on cabin layouts. But McDonnell Douglas's proposition for a short/medium-range airliner with unducted fans (rear-mounted jet engines driving aerodynamically-advanced props) remains of considerable interest to BA; as does the longer-term possibility of such engine technology being applied to the underwing positions on a futuristic Boeing 747; as does the development by Bombardier, of Canada, and Short Brothers, of Belfast, Northern Ireland, to build the RJ, a 50-seater jet for regional routes; as do many other ideas, both starters and non-starters, from the imaginative brains of airframe, engine, avionics and aerospace-equipment design teams.

Quiet operation of new airliners is obviously of considerable interest, for a trade-off for not disturbing the peace around airports could be permission to move landings and take-offs into the present curfew hours, so utilising the aircraft fleets more efficiently, and taking the pressure off crowded airways, runways and terminals. It may be a faint hope, but the aerospace industry, under pressure from the world aviation regulatory bodies, has made big and expensive strides in quietening jet engines over the past decade. However, there are only minimal indications of those who run the aviation infrastructure making returns in kind.

BA's planners have looked at hydrogen-powered aircraft and all the other exotics which are being promoted, but remain unimpressed at this stage. Nor do they believe that any of the several solutions which are being paraded for what will succeed the Concorde supersonic have much to recommend them. Second-generation supersonics will only recoup what would be an astronomical first cost if they could be operated intensely on overland routes. But all the time they produce the sonic boom while they are flying faster than the speed of sound, there is no chance of overland flying being allowed. And nobody looks likely to come up with a technical answer that will kill the sonic boom. And so the Mark 1 Concorde, a major money-earner for BA, will carry on. There is plenty of life yet in that particular aircraft, and with the cosseting which they receive at the hands of BA's engineers, the airline's fleet of seven will still be flying into the twenty-first century.

The final word came from Keith Wilkins, BA's Planning Director and, as such, custodian of the corporate crystal ball. 'The airline industry has its problems, but at any one time there will always be technical advances which will push the barriers further out into the distance. 'Here at BA we continue to be wildy optimistic about the future of air travel.'

INDEX